MW01235622

PEOPLE
DON'T
QUIT
THEIR
JOBS;
THEY
QUIT
THEIR
BOSSES.

BECOME THE LEADER
PEOPLE WANT TO FOLLOW.

JENNIFER-RUTH GREEN

COMBAT VETERAN | ENTREPRENEUR | LEADERSHIP INSTRUCTOR

FOUNDER OF BATTLE-PROVEN LEADERSHIP

KDP Paperback ISBN: 9798865397038
KDP Hardcover ISBN: 9798865397427
Library of Congress Control Number: 2023920674

Published by Battle-Proven Leadership, Crown Point, Indiana.

Written by Jennifer-Ruth Green
Developmental editing by Kimberly McGraw
Editing and proofing by Dr. Sarah Austin and Susan Hobbs
Cover design and layout by Lacey Zarsky

Cleared for open publication on October 31, 2023 by the Department of Defense, Defense Office of Prepublication, and Security Review via reference number: 23-SB-0244.

Although the stories in this book are based on true events, many of the names, locations, and scenarios have been changed to protect the identity and privacy of the individuals involved. The views expressed in this publication are those of the author and do not necessarily reflect the official policy or position of the Department of Defense or the U.S. government. The public release clearance of this publication by the Department of Defense does not imply Department of Defense endorsement or factual accuracy of the material.

Visit battleprovenleadership.com for more leadership resources.

TABLE OF CONTENTS

Dedicated to my Momma.

Thank you for always putting others ahead of yourself as Christ commands. Thank you for caring for Poppa. I love you both.

ACKNOWLEDGEMENTS

This book would not be possible without God. I am thankful for my salvation through Jesus Christ, and the Holy Spirit living within me.

Paul III, Thor, Hector, Jeremy, and Jubilee, I am thankful we are family. I love you...and I'm Mom and Dad's favorite.

Ludwick, thank you for believing that I can.

Lacey Zarsky, your gathered expertise made this a reality.

Kimberly McGraw, without you, this project would have remained merely a thought.

To my Hall of Famers, thank you for your investment in helping me grow.

FOREWORD

The industry of electing people to federal and statewide offices is a highly specialized field that is completely foreign to most Americans, and any familiarity typically comes from shows like "The West Wing" or some similar political drama. It has been my profession for the past two decades, and it has given me a front-row seat to the lack of leadership in American public life. But it is through the election industry that I met Jennifer-Ruth Green–working as her political consultant on her 2022 run for United States Congress.

People often ask why there isn't more leadership in Congress and our state capitals? Democratic government is messy, and the process by which people seek political office is often grueling, painful, and downright ugly. Sadly, many good people with the leadership skills our country needs choose not to put themselves and their families through the wringer. Many of the qualities exhibited by good leaders are in short supply among people who run for office. In fact, often the opposite qualities are encouraged, if not rewarded.

Jennifer-Ruth Green did step up. During a political campaign, you get to know a candidate in a very personal and intimate way–during good times, bad times, and the ups and downs in between. You learn a candidate's strengths and weaknesses and hopes and fears. You see the humanity that doesn't always break through the political advertisements. Jennifer-Ruth was a consummate leader. She is honest and communicates clearly. Her enthusiasm and energy are infectious. She's approachable, relatable, and authentic. And she fights for people, identifies problems, and solves them while building up all the people around her to be leaders.

Battle-Proven Leadership is a clear, concise book that zeroes in on critical leadership skills forged in uniform and in battle, in professional endeavors, and in a high-stakes political campaign. These are leadership lessons for life.

Leadership skills are not inherited. They are learned and maintained through practice, success, and failure, and they are never complete. It is an art, not a science, and Jennifer-Ruth Green has lived a life of leadership.

Tim Edson
Political Consultant

"DO THE BEST YOU CAN UNTIL YOU KNOW BETTER.

THEN, WHEN YOU KNOW BETTER, DO BETTER."

— Maya Angelou

PREFACE

My name is Jennifer-Ruth Green. I serve as a senior U.S. Air Force officer. My résumé includes pilot, CEO, and combat mission commander. I am very proud of the opportunities afforded me throughout my life, but they were never free. In fact, some had steep price tags. All of them shaped who I am, while some altered me completely.

By the time I completed my freshman year at the U.S. Air Force Academy (USAFA), the United States had launched the war on terror, and military members were fighting on two fronts in the Middle East. After I graduated from USAFA, I completed training as a special agent and immediately deployed to Baghdad, Iraq. I served as a counterintelligence officer responsible for leading combat missions outside of our base.

It was an exhausting time (as one might imagine), but nothing felt intolerable until the day an Iraqi guard sexually assaulted me. There are no words to express my emotional state during that time, but I thought I had reached the bottom. I was wrong; the bottom went much deeper.

After my leadership learned of the assault, the situation was poorly handled from the very beginning. My assault was improperly entered into my personnel records (standard protocol is to record the information into my medical records), and now every detail of a devastating and private event was available for others to see. Although there were not many people who had access to my records, I wanted access to be curtailed. Immediately, I followed the proper bureaucratic guidelines, but at the end of a multiyear process, the appeals network determined not to remove this element from my record.

In 2021, I ran for Congress. It was a great time in my life—I met amazing people and felt proud to represent the people in my district. Everything appeared above board as the main contention between my opponent and I was merely philosophical. However, my political opposition hired a firm to scour my military records. This firm acquired my Social Security number and went behind my back, without my knowledge or approval, and posed as my authorized representative in order to obtain my military information. They received my entire personnel file, which included the details of my assault.

Up to that point, no one knew of the assault other than close friends. I fully expected that it would be my choice as to whether I shared this nightmare or not. I decided not to tell my family because I did not want to hurt them. However, members of the national news media—despite my pleas to cease and desist—decided to share it publicly.

This news story reignited the darkest moments of my life and immediately became a national political wildfire. As I tried to make sense of the turmoil that surfaced, the world seemed to move a million miles an hour. By this time in my campaign, I was eighteen months into an incredibly grueling daily routine and I had no capacity or opportunity to stop and address the pain within myself. I had no option but to keep pressing forward.

From the outside, people saw a determined professional, but on the inside, I was reeling and shocked to my core. Of course, I used my rights to request information about exactly how this event occurred. In response to my request, the military mailed me a letter. As I opened it, I expected to understand the who, what, when, and where of the inappropriate release of my files. I needed to know how an institution charged with guarding our country's secrets could have allowed a breach of this nature to happen. As I read the letter, it merely confirmed what I already knew—my records were in the wrong hands.

Overall, the letter was routine and filled with little care or concern. The entire process added insult to injury. I needed someone in the process to see and express that they understood how much of a life-changing debacle this was. Instead, I felt as if the institution was only concerned about closing the loop on the process, neglecting to see me as a teammate who had committed two decades to the mission. As I folded the letter and put it back in the envelope, I felt no relief. I saw that the attempt to "resolve" this situation was not a personal effort by the signatory, but was merely a checkbox on a "to-do" list.

Why do I tell this story? Not because I see myself as a victim, and not because I feel any bitterness. Admittedly, the situation was very difficult, but it led me to consider how I would have handled a situation where one of my colleagues experienced great difficulty. Would I callously treat the situation as an administrative task, or could I see through the red tape to the human being behind the paperwork? I thought of the best leaders with whom I had served, the ones I would follow to the ends of the earth. I realized the common thread was that I always felt valued. I never felt as if I were an item on their "to-do" list.

This truth lit a flame in me, which led me to start a leadership training company, Battle-Proven Leadership, and to write this book. I want to practically help leaders understand how to convey value to those they are leading. People are our greatest asset. Every business and every team is made up of people—real human beings who deserve to feel valued and inherently want to do their best. As leaders, it is our job never to forget the humanity of those with whom we serve. As a company we can produce the best products, but if we overlook their personhood, our colleagues become nothing more than cogs in a machine— replaceable and inhuman.

This book represents a culmination to date of leadership lessons I have learned. My desire is to be vulnerable as I share best practices learned from successes and failures as a leader and as a follower.

Maya Angelou says, "Do the best you can until you know better. Then, when you know better, do better."[1] My hope is that this book allows you to both know and do better. I want you to walk away with renewed confidence as you step into your role each day. I want you to be confident in the value you bring to the team, confident in the culture you set, and confident in the strategies necessary to become a leader worth following.

---

1   (Angelou and Winfrey 2015)

LEADERSHIP FUNDAMENTALS

INTRODUCTION TO LEADERSHIP

CHAPTER 1

LEADERS CONVEY VALUE WHEN...

THEY IMPLEMENT LEADERSHIP PRINCIPLES TO BUILD THEIR TEAM.

1. INTRODUCTION TO LEADERSHIP

Is it true that great leaders are born, not made? Or is that simply a stigma that keeps countless would-be leaders from taking their places in society due to feelings of inadequacy?

The truth is that leadership can be learned. **Leadership is an art**, and the best leaders continually hone their craft. Whether through a mentor or self-education, anyone can learn—and emulate—the principles of effective leaders. Just like any other type of art, the more you practice, the better you become.

Once a person is placed in a leadership role, they must understand the gravity of the role and the internal work it requires. Leadership is not a mask worn when you punch in and taken off as you punch out. It is a mindset shift. After you adopt a leadership role internally, you can then put into practice the philosophy of good leadership.

Effective leadership causes the entire company to be more motivated and loyal, less distracted, and better prepared to scale up. Everyone wins when leaders get better.

As you begin this transformative journey to level up your leadership, it is necessary to define the building blocks of leadership.

Leader | Manager | Team

Leading and Managing Require Two Different Skill Sets

For far too long, the words "leader" and "manager" have been interchangeable, but the concepts can be mutually exclusive. The only requirement to being a leader is that someone is following you. Managers, on the other hand, manage tasks. They monitor a process for an expected outcome. It is important to note that a manager may not necessarily be a leader. Simply put…Leaders lead people. Managers manage tasks.

A Manager Who Manages People as If They Are Tasks Will Be Highly Ineffective

I love hot sauce. As I imagine my favorite condiment being quality-control checked on the assembly line, I see hot sauce is poured to fill the bottles, caps are placed and tightened, labels are attached to bottles, and someone ensures that every part of that process is correct. When the manager inspects a bottle, she goes down the list checking all the boxes to ensure they are complete. "Hot sauce filled to the correct level, check. Label placed correctly, check. Cap twisted on and bottle sealed, check. Good bottle!" If she finds a cracked bottle or skewed label, she sets it aside or tosses it. And on and on she goes all day long.

Sometimes we think we can manage people the same way, treating time management as a "process" that needs to be checked off on a checklist. "Bill was on time, check. Jeff was on time, check. Jack was late...." And whether we take a mental note or literally bring Jack into the office to "lay down the law" it results in treating Jack like a process. A manager would say, "Hey, this is the third time that you're late. This is wrong. You need to do better," and send him right back into the workroom.

Conversely, a leader leads people. A leader understands that Jack is not a process, he is a person. Thus, Jack would have the opportunity to state the problem. "There's a situation going on at home. I'm having issues with my wife and we're separating. I haven't stayed at my house for a week, so I rented an apartment on the other side of town. Since I still have to take my kids to school, my commute is an extra twenty minutes in the mornings."

After gaining further insight, the leader can offer practical solutions. Perhaps Jack can start his shift a little later and make up that time in the evening until things at home calm down. Imagine Jack's response if, instead of being chewed out, he is provided with a reasonable solution. In all likelihood, his respect for the leader and his loyalty to the company will increase exponentially.

The best leaders in my life led me as a person. Here are a few leaders I respect, and the traits that stand out to me about their example:

My father, SMSgt Paul R. Green Jr., instills confidence in people. My mother, Vivian Green, serves with every ounce of her being. Pastor John Wilkerson leads by example, and Mrs. Linda Wilkerson leads with compassion. General Ondra Berry builds other leaders and his belief in people makes them believe they can do anything. General Michael Stohler leads with compassion. General

John Teichert provides customized leadership. General Dana Nelson prioritizes humanity. Colonel Kyle Noel cares about people. Colonel Tami Saylor challenges others to grow.

Take a quick assessment. Spend 10 minutes here naming the best leaders in your life and the reasons why they earned that title. My list illustrates those leaders in my life who conveyed my value to me. They made me want to be a part of the team that they were building, and they made me feel like I would be a valuable member of their team. Employees want to know that they are part of a team, that their opinion matters, that their work matters and that they are helping complete the mission.

The word "team" is the next focal point. When I ask people to define the word team, most often I hear something like, "A team is a group of people who work toward the same goal or have the same purpose," or, "A team is a group of people who wear the same uniform." I can tell you from personal experience in combat that a group of people assigned to work together can have the same goal and wear the same uniform, but still fail to function as a team. Even when lives are on the line, groups of people can be dysfunctional.

The difference between a group of people committed to the same task and a team boils down to one attribute: trust. A group of people who trust one another will want what is best for others, even if that requires self sacrifice. There are stories of people jumping on grenades to ensure the bomb blast radius stays contained so that others live. People who survived these feats of courage often reflect on the fact that they would do it again, commenting that such a choice is simply what their teammates would have done for them if the situation had been different. While a life-and-death scenario in a corporate setting is hopefully something never to be experienced, it is evident that trust is the clear defining characteristic of a team.

Let's return back to the example of Jack, our colleague who showed up late for work. If Jack did not trust his boss, the likelihood that Jack provides an honest, personal explanation for his repeated latenesses is low. If, however, Jack trusts his boss to view him as a person rather than as a task to be managed, or a cog in a wheel, then Jack is more likely to be honest about his personal life, which is why he's late. As a leader, you have the opportunity to establish Jack as a trusted teammate, or alienate him and lose him as a teammate. It is all dependent on how you build trust.

Leaders Build Trust by Conveying Value

When people understand their value, they internalize that they matter. They trust that you have their best interest at heart. This recognition leads to them reciprocating trust. Replicate personal value with each team member, and ultimately everyone is committed to serving the best interests of the group. Conveying value leads to building trust, which leads to building effective teams.

The practical art of leadership is conveying value, which is the key to building mutual trust.

FIGHT FOR YOUR PEOPLE

CHAPTER 2

LEADERS CONVEY VALUE WHEN...

THEY RECOGNIZE THEIR DECISIONS IMPACT MORE THAN THE IMMEDIATE SPACE AND TIME.

2. FIGHT FOR YOUR PEOPLE

My military experience shaped not only my professional life, but also my leadership philosophy. The military showed me that extraordinary leaders fight for their people. In the corporate setting, you may ask, "But who are our people? Who fits within our scope of leadership?" I believe the following story may help answer those questions.

In 2009, I deployed to Baghdad, Iraq. During the greater part of that year to prepare me for the mission, several other counterintelligence agents and I went through extensive physical training and focused on our responsibility to vet and recruit spies. One course I attended was called, "Evasion and Conduct After Capture." In it, we learned how to conduct ourselves in our enemy's presence and how to return with honor. Cadres trained us in escape methods and concepts, as well as how to prepare our families for what could come our way. I remembered a sign I saw overhanging a weight room, which said something like, "Right now, your opponent could be training harder than you." The thought fueled me to work harder.

As we readied for our assignments, some combat, and some support, my thoughts went often to the brothers and sisters in arms who had gone before me, and the friends who lost their lives fighting in this war:

Special Agent Matthew Kuglics recruited and vetted spies to further American interests. Shortly after returning from one deployment, he volunteered to return overseas again to fill a military need. Matt lost his life when the enemy detonated an Improvised Explosive Device (IED).

Captain Mark McDowell was my Air Force Academy classmate turned F-15 pilot, whose smile spread so wide you could see his molars. A great soccer player and brilliant physics major, he tragically died in Afghanistan in a plane crash.

1Lt Roslyn "Roz" Schulte was a year behind me at USAFA. She was incredibly smart and was one of the most kindhearted people I have ever known. She was a standout cadet militarily and was selected to serve in the most senior leadership role awarded to a cadet during their junior year. After graduation, she completed training as an intelligence officer, and deployed to Afghanistan where she lost her life to an IED.

It's frustrating to not be able to give you a full picture of the best of the best that we have lost. To those who did not know these people personally, perhaps these are just names on a page, but to me, and many others, these remain incredibly admirable people who contributed greatly to the task at hand.

Summarizing George Orwell, Richard Grenier once said, "People sleep peaceably in their beds at night only because rough men stand ready to do violence on their behalf."[2] My family could rest well at night because these friends, and many others, kept war at bay. America had infrastructure because no one had bombed the streets. They could go to the hospital because the hospital was still standing. Our government could still operate, produce exports, print useful money, and conduct safe elections...all because people stood and kept violence at bay—people like my friends, Matt, Mark, and Roz.

Now it was my turn to go to war, and foremost in my heart were the people for which I was going to war: my family, my friends, my colleagues. My fellow airmen had already gone to war and returned, and now it was their turn to sleep peacefully in their beds while I stood ready to do violence on their behalf. I was going to war for those I knew and loved, and that was my personal introduction to the concept of where the boundaries lie for how far my leadership extends. I realized a leader must...

Fight for Those You Know

While in Baghdad serving as a mission commander, an Iraqi English teacher shared his story with me. He explained how he had been working with the Americans for years, providing information so we could effectively meet our objectives.

When Al-Qaeda assumed this man was working with us, they tracked him, and fortunately for him, right before they kidnapped him, he ditched all of the identifying paperwork U.S. forces had provided him. For three days, they tortured and interrogated him. All the while, he maintained he was only an English teacher, and they finally released him, believing his cover story.

A couple of years later, they kidnapped his teenaged daughter as she returned home from a study session with friends. U.S. forces worked to locate where the enemy was holding her, and she reunited with her family after Al-Qaeda learned of our imminent raid on their facility. After reuniting with her family,

---

2   Richard Grenier, "Perils of Passive Sex," The Washington Times, April 6, 1993.

they learned just how changed she was physically and emotionally and how she would never be the same in either of those areas ever again.

As I listened to his stories, I had to ask him why would he risk his life and the lives of his family members to help America? He said it was because he believed in a better Iraq, and he believed Americans could help make it so.

His response blew me away. I was fighting for Ros, Matt, and Mark, for my family and friends—and here he was, believing in a bigger scope, a better country for him and his people. What a perspective!

It helped me realize that not only was I responsible for fighting for the people I know, but also the people I did not know. There were millions of Iraqis I did not know who deserved something better. This English teacher believed they were worth fighting for and was willing to give everything—up to and including his life. He believed in something far greater than himself. A leader must...

Fight for Those You Do Not Know

When I came home from war, people would ask me about it, and I would tell them the truth. Combat was the ugliest thing I have ever experienced; it changes you. And for years after I returned home, it continued to affect me. Nagging questions disturbed my peace: Did any of it make a difference? Did it matter?

Sitting in church a few years after I returned from combat, my pastor introduced a visiting pastor from Iraq and invited him to give a report. With interest, I watched the Iraqi pastor climb the altar steps and position himself behind the pulpit. He swallowed as he looked over the congregation, gripped the sides of the podium, then broke down into emotional sobs that echoed through the auditorium. When he composed himself enough to speak, he whispered these words: "I want to thank America, for without you, I could not worship freely."

He explained how, under the dictatorship of Saddam Hussein, there was only one faith. Now, he was free to choose what he believed. He had converted to Christianity, and was permitted to use mass media to share his beliefs. He expressed the honor it was to be used by God in such a way and thanked us for making it possible.

As I listened to the pastor speak so passionately, the emotional weight I had been carrying was released. All the questions in my mind were wiped away with a guttural sigh of relief.

Yes, I fought for the people I knew, but now I understood that I also fought for the people I did not know. The Iraqi pastor's congregation would never know my name, but because we fought for Iraqi freedom, I know I made an impact on their lives. That knowledge comforted me and was what I had been missing. A leader must...

Fight for Those Who Will Never Know Your Name

How does this translate to our everyday working life? As leaders, we must consider the scope of leadership. It is not merely about us and our objectives, but rather we must ensure the well-being of those well outside of our immediate timeline.

Fight for those you know. These are the people who work alongside you and share their needs with you. If it has been a long week and people need to take time off, fight for that. If someone on your team needs more maternity leave or money for newer machines, recognize this and fight for it. Fight for them.

Fight for those you do not know. These are the people who work in your building or company, who you supervise, but may never get to spend a large amount of personal time with. They are the people who do not have an assigned parking spot. They are the people earning minimum wage at your company. Fight for them. Fight for the people who do not have the opportunity to sit in the room and fight for themselves. That is our responsibility as leaders.

Fight for those who will never know your name. One hundred years from now, most likely no one in your company will remember you. But your decisions today will impact their tomorrow. Perhaps you create a lactation room, start paternity leave, or make the building more ADA-compliant. If you consider this concept, decades from now you can rest assured that you will have fought for these people as well.

Truly successful leaders fight for their people, but they understand that leadership extends beyond the immediacy of the current timeframe and their current sphere of influence. They actively work toward creating positive change for all parties.

SHAPE THE CULTURAL ENVIRONMENT

CHAPTER 3

LEADERS CONVEY VALUE WHEN...

THEY SET THE TONE AND FOSTER A POSITIVE CULTURE.

3. SHAPE THE CULTURAL ENVIRONMENT

In the military, whenever I assumed a leadership position over a unit, I would ask my boss about his or her focal areas and goals for the team. Beyond being technically competent and accomplishing the mission in wartime and in peace, what did they want for the unit? I will never forget the story one of my bosses told me about a colossal failure to create a positive culture.

A commander came into a unit after transitioning from the enlisted ranks to the officer ranks. She was known for being a good doer. Once she became a military commander, she struggled. Oftentimes she looked less than sharp, wearing an ill-fitting uniform that sagged and looked sloppy. Immediately, she failed. She was not wearing the uniform the way a commanding officer is expected to wear one and did not convey pride in her appearance. Later that day, that same commander's team member and fellow supervisor, confided that he was currently struggling with a drinking problem and family issues. The commander acknowledged the situation, but shockingly, at the end of the day she announced her selection for the monthly unit-wide morale event: a rum tasting at her favorite bar. Needless to say, the senior team member, and other teammates in whom they had confided, were discouraged and angry.

This commander was so out of touch with her people and the need for a culture of trust that she created a negative environment. Her team found it difficult to respect a commander who did not take their struggles seriously. Had she taken the time to consider what she wanted for her team and the steps needed to get there, she might have made a different decision, and because no one knew about the event prior to her announcement, she could have cancelled it without anyone being the wiser. She could have even rescheduled the event to a later date, but by publicly declaring the invitation so closely to hearing this information from a member of her inner circle, she missed an opportunity to convey that she valued her colleague, their family, and the struggle that they were striving to overcome.

Here are a few thoughts on how to shape the environment.

How healthy is your team culture? If you do not know how to answer that question, consider this one: How do people feel in the pit of their stomach the evening before they return to work? What is your demeanor in the workplace? Do you enter your place of work with a scowl, a warning to anyone who might try to approach you? Does your team walk on eggshells when you are on site? Are you approachable? What is the current work environment you are setting? Do you listen? Your routine disposition will determine how people respond to you.

Leaders are responsible for shaping the culture of a company. When you create a calm environment with a harmonious relationship between the leadership and people, then you develop a group of people who trust one another. You develop a team.

Determine How the Culture Looks

It is common knowledge that people are not overly inclined to "speak truth to power," where people will tell people who can impact change, the truth about the situation. People fear retribution and attribution. One way leaders get around this issue is to conduct anonymous surveys. People feel free to provide their opinions if no one will know it was them.

One way to build confidence in these surveys is to debrief the results to the team. Share what you learned as a result of the survey, and how you intend to improve the environment as a result of what you've learned. This step will breed confidence in people providing feedback.

Remember, you do not have to serve your people in a vacuum. The problems facing organizations are not new, it is merely the context that must be evaluated to determine the most effective solution. Ask other leaders in your industry for how they would solve a similar issue. Be transparent about the issues you face as a leader.

If there is not a clear and apparent group of people with whom you can connect with to discuss this info, create your own. I had the privilege to sit in on a group of IT Leaders connecting for this exact purpose. They introduced the purpose of their gathering as a place where people, "questioned the question." Instead of people bringing their self-identified and implemented solutions to the table, these leaders brought issues and ideas. When they presented their situations to the group, the other participants were responsible for determining if they had asked the proper question to identify the root issue of their problem. It is easy to determine the right answer, but the challenge exists with ensuring you ask the right question.

Let's reflect back on the commander who invited her team for a collective rum tasting. If she asked the group if a rum tasting was a proper morale event, I do not believe she would get much opposition. However, the proper question is, "Why were my senior leaders upset with the morale event I chose?" That would lead her to recognize that her place and time were the detriment causing a lack of cohesion and trust within her unit.

Bottom line, how do you know you are getting effective and timely feedback? You build trust with people so they WANT to tell you the truth when you ask. Eventually, as you continue to build trust you will find that people will tell you the truth BEFORE you ask.

Accept Responsibility for the Present Atmosphere

Good or bad, you need to own responsibility for the current state of your culture. If something is missing, replace it. If there's a need, fill it. As a leader, you do not have the luxury to sit back and complain about the problem—always seek ways to improve it.

If the commander had a desire to make a difference, she would have apologized to her colleague for her insensitive invitation. She then might have said, "Hey, if you need to go get some help or need time off, whatever it is, I can help adjust your schedule and accommodate."

This approach to leadership would have set this commander up for success not just as a leader, but in gaining the respect of her entire team. From there, the culture would grow and flourish because her people would trust that she had their best interests at heart.

What you value, you will propagate. I want an environment that values the family unit. So, when my family calls, I always answer the phone. If able, I balance invitations and activities around my family's schedule to ensure they have the priority. I communicated a clear policy that an excusal for a major family event would aim to be approved. Encourage your teammates to do the same.

Set up activities where the team can invite their families, have "bring your kids to work days," or offer tours of your business. These actions show respect for family while enhancing the family's view of their loved one's job. This is just one example, but you can apply it to anything: self-care, vacations, or flexible work hours. Whenever possible, find what you and your people value and make them key elements in your company's culture.

Promote Unity among Your Colleagues

The biggest way to alienate someone is to disrespect their boundaries. If you are taking a picture with someone, ask permission before you put your arm around them. If someone on your team is struggling with alcohol, and you want to connect with them, choose a place where they will not be tempted to compromise their values.

Encourage friendships in the workplace while discouraging cliques. Be mindful of "jokes" that are targeted or distasteful. Be on the lookout for negative behavior from disgruntled employees when someone gets a promotion.

David Jeremiah in *Searching for Heaven on Earth* said, "People who study the corporate workplace say that interpersonal problems are far more time-consuming than technical problems."[3]

You can't be everywhere all the time and you certainly do not want to parent your team. Head off negative behavior and promote unity in the ranks.

Within any organization, the emergence of cliques is probable; however, few things possess the ability to alienate colleagues faster. Newcomers onboarding to the team will have a more difficult time adapting and identifying what strengths they bring to the table if they are treated as outsiders or not invited into the throng.

One instance in my career where I faced team separation was as a military commander. There were seven operating sections within the unit, and one section was a tight knit group who wanted to create their own sub identity. They developed their own patch and wore it instead of the unit patch. They put blinds up on their office doors and largely kept them closed. They went to lunch together as a group. Their cohesion was exactly what I wanted the rest of the unit to exhibit, as a whole, but not as parts of the whole. My Chief Enlisted

---

3   (Jeremiah 2004)

Manager shared with me that teammates outside of that section were frustrated with the siloing, and ultimately that sub-sect's behaviors were a distraction.

The leader of that section needed to hear that while he had good intentions, his actions were negatively impacting the large unit and potentially, the mission. I delegated the task of discussing this issue to his immediate supervisor. I asked the supervisor and the Chief to discuss a recommended way ahead. One recommendation was for me as the commander to provide a direct order telling the section leader to remove the patches and keep the shop doors open, but I felt the approach was too strong-handed, as a direct order is the strongest tool in a commander's toolkit. Disobedience can result in being held liable under the Uniform Code of Military Justice (UCMJ). I shared with the Chief and the immediate supervisor that the section leader is a leader in our organization and needs to understand the intent and structure behind how the sub-sect's actions had become a distraction. I decided to have the supervisor convey that the unit patch unites the unit and separates us from other units, and allows our whole unit to be a team. Having another, different patch for a small group, undermined that whole-unit collegiality and left teammates feeling ostracized. Ultimately, the conversation was successful, and the approach allowed this section leader to not only comply, but understand the rationale behind the decision.

Be Considerate

A selfless, considerate team player is a person we all value. But those people are atypical, and there are so many things we do without thinking that translate negatively. Here is one commonplace occurrence: if you are heading to your car and see a shortcut through the nicely manicured grass, do you cut across, or stay on the sidewalk even though it means you have to walk farther?

A true team player will take the extra time to follow the sidewalk because they respect the work of others. They respect that someone landscaped that lawn and created a clean path to walk on. A team player will focus on the company's reputation and will want the workplace to look presentable.

Another way to show respect is encouraging collaboration and showing courtesy between departments. Many times, it can be an "us vs. them" mentality, when it really should be everyone doing what they can to reach the goal. At some point, one department is going to struggle, and it will be that much harder to get things done if drama is allowed to go unchecked.

So much of leadership requires seeing into someone else's world and responding accordingly. When you are conscious of others, it translates into respect and your team will respond in kind.

Use the word "team" as often as possible. In emails or in every-day language, write it or say it. This practice helps to reinforce the team culture you want to develop and is one clear pathway to inviting people to become a part of the team. It also allows them to believe they are part of the team.

All of the above are methods to develop and maintain a sound culture, but what do you do if your work environment is less than ideal? How do you go about making the necessary changes?

Funnel Changes Strategically

Start with your immediate colleagues. Decide what you want to propose and take it to the group of people that you work closest with and say, "This is an idea I have, and this is how I think it will help. What are your thoughts?" The reason it is so important to get the top leaders on board with our vision is because we want the information to funnel properly. When everyone is on board with the vision, it makes for an ideal transition in procedure.

It is important they are on board with these changes because they will be the ones implementing them. Stay in that meeting until you and your team have thrown out all the bad ideas and accepted the good ones. Then, when everyone has a full understanding, say, "Okay, let's drive this out to the mid-level managers."

After the next tier of management not only hears it, but aligns with it, the concept will funnel down with clarity. Any lack of clarity is cleared up when a supervisor allows their subordinates to ask questions and convey challenges to the plan, or think through execution limitations.

When we give our leaders direction, they ought to believe in it so much that they say, "This is what we are doing," not "This is what the boss wants." If they do not buy into the plan or are doing it merely because we want them to, then we have failed as leaders. It is our responsibility to ensure everyone is on the same page.

When I ran for Congress, one of my first meetings with my small team of three began with us trying to effectively articulate my "why." I had to determine why I was running, convey it to the team, and figure out how to package it for my constituents. Every issue I was concerned about revealed that our district deserved better than the governance we were receiving. We decided on the campaign's vision: "Hoosiers Deserve Better." I identified focal areas and knew I needed a passion as I would be spending a lot of time and energy connecting with people about them. The areas were: strong families, strong economy, and strong national security. I needed to learn about the most effective methods of strengthening those areas on a national scale.

I needed to learn how to communicate my vision effectively to the masses. I took media training weekly and before all major appearances. I gave speeches and spoke to thousands of people, sharing my vision of how we could achieve better. The team was focused on making sure every decision/event/speech/call was centered around our rationale. If someone wanted me to give a speech about education or agriculture, we would accept the opportunity only if it did not conflict with another opportunity to speak on the focal areas. We had our priorities organized and were working to ensure we were focused.

The effort to convey my vision to the masses was important, but most important was conveying it to the team. As the team grew, I needed to lead and reinforce my vision. My core team expanded from three to ten and I knew that if these ten people, who represented me across finance, events, scheduling, communications, and outreach, did not get the message, then the 350,000+ people we needed to vote for us, would not get it either. Vision is incredibly important.

New Leaders Should Implement Major Changes Only When Necessary and Always Cautiously

In a new role, it's important to assess your situation before you make any major changes. I would suggest that you wait a few months to make any adjustments on elements that do not require immediate changes. Sometimes, change is unavoidable. If it is illegal, immoral, unethical, or another emergency situation, you will need to step in and make the call, but if it is less serious or simply a personal preference, I would encourage you to put it on hold. For many people, change alone can be unnerving, warranted or not. That anxiety is compounded when you have not built mutual trust.

There is often a period of time needed to adjust your focus to include all aspects of the business in your decisions. The last thing you need as a new leader is to alienate the people on your team because of a wrong or poorly executed decision.

A CEO I know exercised this philosophy with a company he took over during an intensely chaotic situation. Though his natural inclination may have been to make sweeping and drastic changes, he held off from making any major changes until the employees had time to trust him. For him, this process took a year.

I came to appreciate this style of leadership later when I witnessed a lower-level supervisor take over one of the departments and obliterate it. She saw much that needed to be improved, and in the employees' view, haphazardly implemented sweeping policy changes without accounting for long-term negative effects. Needless to say, this style alienated her from many of her teammates, and her tenure lasted less than two years before she "resigned."

LEADERSHIP FUNDAMENTALS

IDENTIFY AND SOLVE PROBLEMS

CHAPTER 4

LEADERS CONVEY VALUE WHEN...
THEY ELIMINATE DISTRACTIONS.

4. IDENTIFY AND SOLVE PROBLEMS

In the complex machinery of a business, leadership is the central cog. How effective that cog performs with the others depends on our capabilities as a leader. You may have heard the phrase "everything rises and falls on leadership." We may know our businesses inside and out, but that knowledge is useless if we cannot communicate our vision, cannot build trust, and thus, are not a leader people want to follow.

One aspect of leadership is accepting accountability for every part of our business, both the good parts and the bad parts. It is easy (although not the best practice) to accept accolades for successful or high yields, but, it is important to accept responsibility when mishaps occur or productivity is not at its peak. It doesn't matter what fell through the cracks. The responsibility is ultimately on us, and we need to accept that.

When we lead with a desire to serve people, our teammates will allow us to serve them. People expect to bring problems to the boss, and they expect the boss to solve them. You continue to build trust as you produce results in this area.

"The day the soldiers stop bringing you their problems is the day you stopped leading them. They have either lost confidence that you can help them or concluded that you do not care. Either case is a failure of leadership."[4]
— General Colin Powell

One clear measure of whether or not we are effective in our pursuit to eliminate distractions is to see if people bring us their issues. A concept I share with my team is that I cannot solve problems I don't know about. I want them to be proactive in the two-part relationship of us working together to solve issues. On the leader's end, there are several practical techniques to show that we take our responsibility seriously in this area...

---

4   (Powell and Persico 2003)

Take Care of the Problems Your People Cannot Solve

As a young girl, I loved scouring newspaper garage sale ads and mapping a route from one to the next. One day, I noticed an ad for a furniture store offering fabric book racks. I cut out the listing, showed it to my dad, and begged him to take me to get this really cool book rack. Though I'm sure he had many other things on his plate that day, he could tell how excited I was, so he obliged.

When we arrived, I jumped out of the car clutching my newspaper clipping and practically dragged dad into the store. When I showed the picture to the man behind the counter, he barely glanced in my direction. He clearly was not keen on being bothered by a little kid, and he finally muttered something like, "I don't know anything about that." I tried to show him the picture again, explaining that I took it from the newspaper. He could not have cared less.

My dad very calmly said to the man, "Sir, my daughter brought in this advertisement from your company. I think you should take a look in your back room and see if you can't find one."

Stunned that my father stepped in for what he estimated to be such a menial request, the man silently slipped into the back room for a few minutes and returned with the very same cloth book rack from the newspaper clipping. I loved that book rack and kept it for many years. I think the reason why it held such nostalgia was because whenever I looked at it, I remembered that my dad advocated for me when I was too small to do so.

That is what you need to do for your people. When no one hears their voice, use yours. If they need a raise, or more supplies, or better health care to meet the needs of their family, that is what you are there for. If our teams know we have their backs, they feel valued, and they are going to work hard.

When we own problems within our team or organization, we are creating an environment people want to work in. We focus on our people and fight for them. A phrase I use often is simply, "I'll take care of it. Thank you." When you say those words, what you are really saying is, "I really appreciate your feedback and want you to continue to bring me problems that are at my level. You don't have to worry about it anymore." Trust is developed when people believe that you are going to take care of things that they cannot. You handling that problem means they can get back to solely focusing on their assignment.

Leaders might believe that once they are in a role of leadership, their work is done. They get to sit on top and supervise while everyone else works. But if you want to be a leader with an incredible team and a solid cultural environment, then your work is far from over. Greater roles and positions require greater responsibility—not greater rights and privileges. As a leader, you show up every day and earn your paycheck by serving your colleagues.

Have a Degree of Urgency in Getting Problems Solved

Sometimes people will want to move on, and that is okay. Circumstances change, priorities change, family needs change, and people move on. However, as you know from the title of this book, "People don't quit their jobs; they quit their bosses." There may be a time when you, or your culture are the source of their issue. I remember the first time someone "quit me." He shared he wanted to leave; I inquired about why, and he said, "It just isn't fun anymore. It never felt like work before, but every day I wake up, it feels like work." That was the polite answer, but what I understood was that I had taken a culture he had appreciated and enjoyed, and turned it into the opposite of that. It was painful to consider, because several others shared their desire to stay, continue to grow, learn, and teach. They felt valued and interested in the culture that I was building. But the culture I worked to create was not for everyone.

You may have experienced this kind of incompatibility already, or it may be a part of your future. Regardless, work as hard as possible to prevent this from becoming a reality because staff retention is a costly problem for businesses, and frequent turnover can negatively impact team morale. I served in a military unit that had four commanders in three years. Learning new leadership styles, personalities, preferences and priorities led to confusion, frustration, and fatigue. Needless to say, the majority of people in the unit had difficulty throwing immense energy into the mission.

Pay Attention to Why People Transition

Despite your efforts to set a positive work environment, people will still move on to other opportunities. When you do have someone who wants to leave, it is important to conduct an exit interview to determine why. Sometimes they leave because of practical reasons, for example, their spouse took another job in another location and their family is relocating. However, sometimes it does have something to do with the culture, their supervisor, pay—something that was in their boss's control. If the new job is in a similar field as the one they are leaving (as it usually is), what was so attractive that it caused the employee to quit?

Conduct these interviews in person and commit to listening. Do not make it a situation where you are aiming to convince someone to stay. I recommend this because you will be more successful serving alongside people who want to be on your team. If someone admittedly does not want to be there, you are asking someone to transition from uncommitted to fully committed, and expecting it to happen in a relatively short time.

Take notes after the meeting; do not appear distracted by trying to capture information as it comes. When the meeting is over, take the time to write down the major ideas presented. Paying attention allows the person leaving to feel that they are heard and valued. Leave that as a lasting impression on them. Take those notes and reflect on what you could have done better. If something needs a rapid adjustment, for example, if there is a culture of harassment or unequal treatment, make that adjustment swiftly. However, two people having personality differences is something that just happens. Regardless, it is important to think through the experiences your people are having, and determine where you can assist.

We touched briefly on the need to share success and own failure. This mentality and activity can produce some amazing results:

It Fosters a Culture of Honesty

Trust grows when people are honest. Owning mistakes and failures grows trust. When your team trusts you, they are more motivated, productive, fulfilled, and secure in their work environment. Trust creates a culture of transparency that encourages honest dialogue and communication. Instead of shifting blame, employees take a cue from the boss and are more willing to accept responsibility and learn from their mistakes.

A lack of trust can cause tension, create the temptation to hide weaknesses and mistakes, and can have detrimental effects on the success of a business.

It Fosters Open Communication

Leaders who are willing to admit to mistakes allow people to feel comfortable sharing their true opinions and ideas. Conversations are easier to come by, and team members can share ideas and opinions honestly. Ultimately, open communication allows leaders to hear from their team, and understand how to better not only the unit, but themselves.

It Generates Respect and Inspires Loyalty

It is a rare—and truly profound—moment when failure occurs, and a leader sees people as a part of solving the problem, as opposed to the problem themselves. Most often, we are quick to seek a scapegoat for why something went wrong. However, it is important to recognize that people are not intending to fail. Perhaps the system itself is the culprit and needs an overhaul. By asking for a collaborative effort for solutions, people will be inclined to participate in problem solving. Ask, "What could we have done to prevent this from happening? What could I have done earlier to make sure we didn't end up in this situation?"

It Serves as an Incubator for New Leadership

When supervisors take ownership of failures, it creates a safe space for employees to take calculated risks and explore innovative solutions. Team members are more likely to innovate and contribute their ideas when they know they won't be unfairly blamed for any setbacks.

Do you see the pattern? When we take responsibility for the successes and failures of our business, we are leading by example and encouraging our employees to follow. When our people see us humbling ourselves to better our workplace, they will value that effort and partner with us to maintain a thriving culture.

LEADERSHIP FUNDAMENTALS

COMMUNICATE EFFECTIVELY

CHAPTER 5

LEADERS CONVEY VALUE WHEN...

THEY LEARN TO USE THEIR WORDS EFFECTIVELY.

5. COMMUNICATE EFFECTIVELY

Leadership is not just about having the confidence and ability to lead, but also having the wisdom to speak responsibly. Words are free, but if you are careless, they may cost you. Good leaders strive to communicate effectively because they understand the weight their words carry. Here are several principles to follow when you communicate:

Give Clear Instructions

I remember one time I was leading a new team, and I was not clear with my intention to have a brainstorming session. I was sharing thoughts and they had their notebooks out, documenting my every word. They were scribbling ideas, intent, and actions they could take to make sure they met my intent. After a few minutes of ideas which were completely contradictory, I remember a teammate dropped their pen, and asked me with great exasperation, "Ma'am, what exactly do you want us to do?" I was confused because I thought we were all generating ideas. I thought their questions were to help me think, but rather they were to clarify my intent. I realized then that as a leader people will listen with intent to "do."

I should have led with, "I don't need you to take notes, I just want to talk through some ideas." This invitation to close the notebooks would free my team to engage instead of chasing the loose ends of brainstormed ideas. Clear communication means fewer misunderstandings and less wasted time.

If you want a brainstorming session, be clear about it. If you want something specific done or instructions followed, make sure your team knows you are giving a directive. Clear direction saves your people time and frustration and allows them to know how they can best participate.

During a military assignment, I spent three months at the Air Force Academy where I worked with a new team. This became a leadership refresher course since I was starting from scratch, helping to lead a team of people unfamiliar to me.

I worked with a fellow airman on a project that I felt was easy and self-explanatory, but it wasn't long before I saw that he was struggling with understanding how to achieve the intended end state of the task. I tried many different ways to explain what I wanted the end product to look like, but to no avail. He was not on the same page, and no matter how many words I used, nothing seemed to work. I could tell we were both getting frustrated. I was frustrated because I could not leave him with the project that I felt he was more than qualified for, and he was frustrated because he didn't want to appear unable or unwilling to complete tasks.

Finally, I asked another colleague for help. Why was it so difficult for the airman and I to connect on this task? She said that I started with an assumption of knowledge. Instead, she recommended I start from the beginning and explain the end product requirement and its intent. Then, we could walk through the process in its entirety.

I took her advice, and as I walked through my explanation, I could see the light come on in my colleague's eyes. That was when I realized my mistake: I gave instructions from the halfway mark of understanding. I assumed he knew as much about the project type as I did. I failed to meet him where he was and ask how much he knew about the topic overall. I would have discovered far earlier that I needed to define terms.

It would have been easy to become upset after his lack of productivity (it was an easy project in my mind), but I took responsibility for the wasted time and effort because I failed to lead my teammate in a way he understood. When I acknowledged my misstep, I apologized, and we were able to move forward productively. In this case, his work ethic was not lacking, but my communication was. Remember, you cannot hold people accountable if you do not communicate with them in a way they understand.

One tool I recommend is, after giving instructions, ask the question, "Can you share what you understand that I'm asking of you?" Sometimes their feedback is 180-degrees off of the intent, but the question allows me clarification to make sure they understand.

Also, colloquialisms, industry-specific jargon, slang, and ambiguous terms like, "Can you take care of this?" can all impede clear communication. If I praise one of my managers in Mandarin, it doesn't matter how many accolades I offer; if he doesn't speak the language, he's not going to feel appreciated.

One instance where I was on the receiving end of miscommunication as a subordinate led me to feel very frustrated. I had attempted to coordinate an event on my boss's calendar. He called to correct me about how I went about the process. I knew the date and time of the event and went directly to his administrative assistant to ensure the event was scheduled.

My boss scolded, "Please speak with me directly for appointments because if not, my assistant will block that time on the calendar."

What I heard was that my boss wanted me to make the appointments directly with him because he would input the information into the calendar and his assistant would not have to. Why would a senior military officer want to input dates into his own calendar? I accepted the reprimand, but I was confused, and admittedly a bit frustrated.

Before the conversation ended, I said, "Sir, I will always accept constructive criticism, but I do not understand how what I did failed to meet your intent regarding your schedule."

He explained how one of his assistant's responsibilities is to weigh the invitations he receives, and prioritize appointments. If my boss does not explicitly say that an appointment must be added to his calendar, and is a priority, there is a risk of the appointment getting "blocked" from entering the calendar. At that point, it made sense to me. That word "blocked" had different meanings for both of us, and when I sought clarity, I understood my boss's intent and was able to adjust accordingly.

Be Considerate

Be kind and be gracious. Always have a kind word for someone. If they recently did a good job on a project, let them know. Find a way to honestly and genuinely appreciate their person and work. You never know how your kind word will impact someone's day. In fact, your words can change the trajectory of someone's day. When you walk in, try to meet people where they are. A leader I know discusses how he can walk down a hallway and celebrate a major life event with someone, and a few feet later connect with someone grieving a loss. Seeking to meet people where they are will require a lot of emotional intelligence and a lot of effort. As an introvert, when I spend time seeking to truly engage with people where they are, I find that at the end of the day I am emotionally, physically, and mentally exhausted. But, I can rest knowing that people felt valued.

Another way to show gratitude is to buy and write thank-you cards. Whenever I see something that deserves recognition, or when I want to express my appreciation, I take the time to write a short note to the recipient. Every time I write one, the recipient is grateful. It is a small memento of our time together, and allows them to know I value them.

Make Good Decisions

I originally titled this section, "Be decisive" because I wanted leaders to be unafraid of making definitive resolutions. It is clear that one of the most frustrating communication barriers for a subordinate is when the boss is indecisive. When the boss cannot, or will not, make a decision, there is no direction. People do not know the vision, and therefore, action is stalled. However, the more I considered it, the more I realized that while I wanted leaders to make decisions, they had to be good decisions. Thus, I changed the header to qualify the type of decisions we must make. Here are some practical ways to make good decisions:

1. Recognize That Good Is Not Always the Enemy of Best

Sometimes a 90% solution is perfectly fine. An adaptation of Gen. George Patton's quote frequently circulated in the business world is, "A good plan executed today is better than a perfect plan next week." Occasionally, it is simply unwise to wait to receive and review all of the information prior to deciding a course of action. As a leader, it is important to recognize when to gather more information, and when to make a decision based on what you know. There will be times when advancing a project the remaining 10% of the way requires an inordinate amount of human-hours to complete, an excess that's too immense. For instance, when planning a meeting, it is important to collect agenda items from every participant. If one participant is traveling and unable to respond in time to provide the agenda prior to the meeting, it is wiser to forego collecting their inputs and just publish the agenda. The agenda is not 100% complete, but it can be provided to the meeting participants in a timely manner.

2. Strive for Excellence

There are some situations where it's clear that perfection does not have to be achieved; however, do not mistake this recommendation as advocacy for mediocrity. It is important to provide first-class work. As a quick example, on the flightline people will often conduct Foreign Object and Debris (FOD) walks. Everyone will stand shoulder to shoulder and walk along the airplane parking ramp and flightline to grab any items that could be sucked into an aircraft's engine, thereby rendering it inoperational. In this instance, a 90% solution is not acceptable.

3. Understand Indecision Is a Reality

For various reasons, it can be difficult to make a decision. You may have too much information or not enough information. When you are unable to make a decision because you have too much information, ask your team specific questions to clarify the situation so you can make a decision. Allow them to help you pare down the information to the most reasonable elements.

When you do not have enough information to make a decision, be clear with your ask for additional information. If you need definitions, more data, or more specifics about how facts relate to the decision, just ask. People will be more than happy to provide the information within their specialty.

4. Difficulty Assessing the Information

I have had instances when I personally have not been able to make a decision because of analysis paralysis. When I continuously evaluate and reevaluate every option before me, I become stuck, and unable to choose. During this situation, I write down pros and cons to each decision. Then, I reach out to my leadership team, or a mentor, and explain my stuck points and the pros and cons. Then, I ask for their opinion. Often, their inclinations will help break the proverbial tie.

5. Decision Fatigue

Sometimes leaders are physically unable to make a decision because of decision fatigue. They have made too many decisions and eventually their brain becomes tired. For many people, decisions are made as soon as their feet hit the ground in the morning and continue all day. From which clothes to wear and what food to eat, to which road to take to work and which emails to delete, the requirement to make decisions is a stressor for everyone. At some point, making wise decisions is untenable. I try not to make large decisions at the end of the day. I know I am physically and mentally tired, and not at my sharpest. I recommend setting a definite stop to decision-making for the day. I can tell when my brain gets fatigued because I have to read and reread information just to understand it, or I find myself caring less than I usually would about ensuring I am asking the right questions. At that point, it is a wise practice to say internally, "No more decisions until tomorrow." Then, if someone asks for you to make a decision, you can say, "Can we make this decision tomorrow? I want to make a wise decision here and will be more ready to process it then." That way you are proactively addressing their concerns, but allowing yourself time to refresh in order to make a good decision.

6. Mental Health

Another reason leaders are unable to make decisions is because of mental health. Mental health issues like stress, depression, or anxiety greatly impact people's ability to operate at their best. During one very busy season in my life, I had taken on too many projects. I was operating in a space where expectations were high in every area. I was trying to do everything for everyone, and felt the burden and pressure of performance. I became so emotionally, physically, mentally, and socially exhausted that I was unable to do even the simple things.

While completing the run portion of my military physical fitness test, I could not make my legs move up or down. I could not will them to move faster. I had never failed any portion of a physical fitness test before, but because my body was so worn, I was ineffective. I had no capability to overcome any of the internal hindrances. This experience led me to have a clear discussion with my boss because I needed him to know that I was unwell. I needed him to know that I needed rest. I intentionally put aside every requirement and took days to pray, rest, and relax by participating in some of my favorite activities. It was refreshing. One adage I like is, "You need to come apart before you come apart." This saying comes to mind frequently now, and when I feel an inkling of exhaustion, I immediately find time to address recovery.

Communicate in a Timely Manner

A leader I respect shared her philosophy behind organizing her email inbox, specifically sharing her focus on signing documents first. If you are anything like me, when you get in the office every morning, your inbox is flooded with information and information requests. Signing items shows a prioritization of the things that only you can do. Without your signature a process cannot continue. You are actively holding up progress when you do not prioritize this task. You can show that you value your team's work, and time, by limiting ways in which you cease productivity.

Adopt Positive Language

Setting a positive tone in your workplace is an effective way to inspire people to respond and act accordingly. Even if you work in a warehouse where clients never visit, you should still encourage professionalism and positivity.

I understand not every workplace has a professional culture, but that does not mean you should not exhibit one. People will often rise to a higher level of behavior if they see someone they respect leading by example.

One practical example is to phrase terms in the affirmative. For example, when reading an employee rulebook, it's much more pleasant to see, "You are free to eat lunch for an hour anytime between 11:00 a.m. and 1:00 p.m." as opposed to "Your lunch cannot last longer than an hour, you must not leave before 11:00 a.m., and you must return by 1:00 p.m." They both share the same sentiment, but the first instance uses positive language. Review the wording in your employee handbook and see if it conveys positive language.

Be Mindful That a Leader's Words Have an Impact

One day, I walked into work and noticed a new picture hanging on the wall. I thought the picture was a bit high. It was not a big deal, really, but I said the comment out loud and thought nothing more of it.

When I came in the next day, the picture was lower. I went to the person responsible and asked them about the photo. They thought I wanted it moved. This moment caught my attention because I made a comment that I thought meant nothing, but they took it as a directive.

I realized then that my team will do what I say and interpret action from what they think I am saying. Leading is a responsibility we should not take lightly. We should not let our two cents cost the team a dollar, as I did with my offhand comment. Someone drilled new holes and filled in the old ones, which included a trip to the store, sanding, and painting over the filled holes. I cost that employee more than they were planning to spend on something that mattered little to the company because I was not careful with my words.

As leaders, we should be mindful of how we communicate with others and how our words reflect on us personally and professionally. We want our communication to create a positive culture in which our teams can work effectively and efficiently.

PART II
LEADERSHIP & YOU

LEADERSHIP & YOU

RECOGNIZE THE GRAVITY OF YOUR ROLE

CHAPTER 6

LEADERS CONVEY VALUE WHEN...

THEIR CONDUCT MATCHES THEIR WORDS.

6. RECOGNIZE THE GRAVITY OF YOUR ROLE

Joining the Air Force straight out of high school, I had aspirations of serving my country and being the best I could be. I studied hard at the Air Force Academy and trained harder, not knowing that by the end of my freshman year, we would be a nation at war.

When I deployed to Baghdad as a mission commander, beyond the responsibility for the mission, my other primary focus was bringing every teammate back in the same condition they left our Forward Operating Base. This goal was my first real leadership role outside of the Air Force Academy, where we trained in a manufactured environment. I soon found that real life is much different.

At the time I was present, the U.S. government's main objective in Baghdad was to turn over control of the country to the Iraqis. Once they took over security, they locked down most Allied movements. Most personnel could not leave the Forward Operating Bases; however, my unit's primary mission required us to operate outside of the wire.

One such mission came when our chaplains received a generous donation of crayons, coloring books, and toys. They wanted to visit the local prison to extend goodwill to the Iraqi women and children who congregated there. Security forces cleared the roads of improvised explosive devices (IEDs), so my team set out for the city of Baghdad to help pass out the gifts.

There were at least five of us inside the Mine-Resistant Ambush Protected (MRAP) vehicle, silently swaying as we rolled down the city streets. Our team had bonded over twelve-hour days working together and traversing unfamiliar territory when we traveled, talking about home and families. I remember looking at each of them, thinking of their individuality and what they meant to their families and to me. Those few moments of contemplation made me acutely aware of the weight of my role and the responsibility I owed each of my colleagues. No training in the world could prepare someone for the candor of a moment like that.

Also on this mission was a new member of the team, our lead interpreter for that specific mission. He was a native Iraqi turned Army soldier, as he had gained citizenship after moving to New York and joining the U.S. military. It's always difficult for newcomers joining a tight team, and although he and I were paid by the same government, transparently, during the year I spent preparing for this mission, I had developed a sincere distrust for the Iraqi people because I had solidified the entire people group as my enemies.* Now, here I was, tasked with entrusting my life—and the lives of the people for whom I was responsible—to one.

We parked across the street from the prison, twenty yards from the women and children who came to visit their imprisoned men. I instructed our interpreter to let the women know we had gifts and to ask them to line up so we could distribute them. He said something in Arabic. The women looked in our direction, and then all at once sprinted toward us as fast as they could.

The scene turned horrific as they trampled a young child. No one stopped to help him. They kept running at us, dressed in full abayas with only their faces visible. Why were they running? Were they concealing something under their clothes? We were taken completely off guard by the stampede.

The military may have cleared me to be the mission commander, but there was a gravity to this situation I was wholly unprepared for. I did not know these people, and I did not know our interpreter who stood there allegedly relaying my instructions. And I certainly could not fathom what could be so important to these women that they would trample a child.

I commanded my team to climb onto the MRAP and use the vantage point to better assess the situation. Unholstering my weapon, pulling it out and pointing it at the ground, I told the interpreter to make everyone move back. As he issued commands, I stood ready, scanning the crowd for threats. Just then, a little boy caught my attention. Not because of anything he said or did, but for the utter despondency in his eyes. In that look, the realities of war materialized. There stood a little boy, who should be free to laugh and play and live an innocent life but was, instead, standing in the midst of chaos. He did not flinch at the sight of my gun or the ravages of desperation displayed by these women. It broke me.

Standing nine feet in the air, with heat shimmering off the metal vehicle beneath our feet, I could hear the cacophony of frantic voices fade below us.

*Author's note: I feel it important to share that after I returned from combat, I was emotionally hindered by my inner sentiment of mistrust and anger towards the Iraqi people. I spent a significant time interpersonally confronting my bias, and changing my heartset and mindset. Since returning from combat, I have had many peaceful and friendly engagements with the Iraqi people.

The reality of our situation left me stunned. We had been mere seconds from the life-altering decision of firing on a group of women and children.

It was this surreal moment that propelled me to further develop my leadership. Before, during, and after each mission, when I had a minute to think, I processed leadership. What is leadership? What is a team? How am I leading? Who are the people I am leading and how do I motivate them?

As I stood there facing dozens of Iraqi women and children, so many questions swirled in my mind. I knew leadership on the battlefield was not only about keeping your people alive; it was about motivating people to do the things that were needed despite the knowledge that your enemy could be around any corner.

But was I really ready to open fire on people? Who was my target? As a military officer, what was the threat here? Thoughts of the My Lai Massacre ran through my head. Could I justify the use of force? Was I de-escalating as much as I should be? Did I put my people at risk? What did the interpreter tell them? Is this how I am going to die?

As frightened as those questions made me, the situation quickly calmed and, still atop the MRAP, we began handing out the gift bags. The Iraqis took their bags and walked back across the street.

I realized something significant then: I was at war. My teammates were at war. These women were in their home country, just waiting to see their father, brother, cousin, or uncle. They had not started this conflict; they merely wanted it to end.

It was hard not to feel some humanity toward these people, but I could not let that dictate the mission to get my people home. I had to keep my feelings in check and focus on the next task. The realities of war meant that one of those women could decide that the long-term incarceration of her family member deserved retribution. The next time someone ran toward me after one of their countrymen yelled a charged statement, the situation could end differently. I had to remain on guard and ready to make the split-second decisions each unique situation required.

Through that experience, I learned that the words I use as a military officer can cost everybody under my command everything—up to and including their lives. The decisions I make, the words I use, and my conduct must allow people to build confidence and trust in each other as a team. A group of people who trust one another can do amazing things.

I understand you might not face life-and-death situations in your leadership role, but your decisions still affect lives: The lives of those who work for you, the lives of their spouses, the lives of their children, and even the lives of those your followers encounter. On your best days, worst days, and every day in between, your actions and speech affect the people around you. The gravity of that thought should lend itself to a greater reflection on personal conduct and preparation.

MASTER FOUR ELEMENTS OF LEADERSHIP

CHAPTER 7

LEADERS CONVEY VALUE WHEN...

THEY ADOPT A COMPREHENSIVE WORLDVIEW AND STRIVE FOR PURE MOTIVES.

7. MASTER FOUR ELEMENTS OF LEADERSHIP

There are four elements every leader must refine:

- Toolset
- Skillset
- Mindset
- Heartset

The first two are common and found among leaders and doers alike. The last two are the elements I want to emphasize in this chapter. We often undervalue the impact that a clear worldview and proper motive have in today's leadership, but they remain a vital ingredient in the recipe for success.

Toolset: A Basic Knowledge of the Required Elements of Your Job

These are the basic skills you carry with you as a result of your craft. If you are a builder, it is the knowledge of how to build a house. If you are a doctor, it is memorizing the different bones in the body. If you are a soldier, it is understanding how to fight, how to stay alive, and how to perform your duties. These are the foundational elements. Everyone brings a basic toolset to be able to do their job.

Examples of a doer's toolset:
- Basic knowledge
- Physical tools
- Required licenses

A Doer's Skillset: The Practical Training You Use to Optimize the Tools in Your Toolkit

It is a builder who doesn't just build a house, but someone who builds a well-crafted house. It is a doctor who has expertise in a particular life-and-death scenario. It is a soldier who trains not only to stand in formation, but to discern when someone is holding something back in an interrogation scenario. Your toolset is the basic knowledge. Your skillset is the level at which you utilize your tools.

Examples of a doer's skillset:

- Experience using the tools
- Ability to train people
- Adaptability in various situations
- Problem-solving capabilities
- Ability to inspire people when they communicate

Every "doer" has a foundational toolset and a skillset, but leaders exhibit, exercise, and grow in the next two elements: mindset and heartset.

A Leader's Mindset: The Worldview from Which You View Your Responsibility

As a leader, do you recognize the reality of the world in which you are operating? Are you focused on what you can gain? Are you focused on who your people are and how to communicate with them? Do you understand your environment and the true task at-hand of conveying value and building trust?

While in Baghdad, a group of five soldiers and I took a civilian to meet one of our sources. After parking, some of us set up a perimeter while the rest of us readied to escort the woman to her destination.

Everyone was armed and watchful, ready to protect our civilian in the event anyone launched an attack on our exposed party. We fully expected her to be cognizant of the situation, but upon stepping from the armored vehicle, she stood outside in the sun, stretched, complained about being cooped up, and then commented on how desperately she needed to tan.

There we were, fully exposed to enemy combatants, and she was completely unaware of the situation. This woman's worldview did not consider that everyone was there to protect her or that we were at war. She had no clue how much time we spent briefing and coordinating the mission. Her worldview focused on herself and her agenda. It did not match the reality of the situation and put every one of us in danger.

As leaders, we must understand our worldview and how it affects our team. If your people see you are only concerned with the immediate and do not understand the reality of your business, they will not follow you.

Remember the commander who invited her unit to a rum tasting? She thought she was providing an expensive and enjoyable outing for her team, but her narrow worldview rudely disregarded her teammate's struggle with alcohol and in turn limited her influence with her team. It also eroded her team's trust in her leadership.

She should have been someone her team could respect. Someone whose intuition they could trust. Someone they would be willing to follow into combat. Her worldview should have included her team and their needs.

A good leader has knowledge of the process and can identify a good product. But they transition from a doer to a leader by gaining a proper heartset and mindset. They focus on the business while also knowing what their people are dealing with on a day-to-day basis.

If you are a leader who struggles with awareness and a narrow worldview, grow your mindset. Some personalities are naturally more empathetic than others, but regardless of whether you are "good at it" or not, you have people in your realm of influence who can lend perspective and help you expand your mindset. You can also learn to connect with people more effectively by reading books, attending leadership conferences, or listening to podcasts. Ideally, you will transition from managing products and quality control to focusing on the company's mission and leading the people you have the privilege of serving.

A Leader's Heartset: Your Motives and Why You Do What You Do

During one job search I received offers from two different bosses. The jobs were similar and paid similarly, but one boss was interested in what I brought to the team while the other's primary focus was on how this role would help me grow as a person in order to meet my end goals. Any guess as to which boss I chose to work for? It was an easy "yes" to work for the boss who conveyed that my goals had value to him. A leader who leads with pure motives and is focused on bringing value to their team, is a leader worth following.

These leaders have passion and purpose for what they do and understand the gravity of their responsibility. Effective leaders utilize their influence to develop people rather than exploiting them for their own gain. Often we find leaders who are self-absorbed, greedy, and/or consumed by climbing the corporate ladder; however, to paraphrase Mahatma Ghandi's quote…

Leadership Begins When the Power of Love Overrules the Love of Power

Your toolset and skillset are important because they give you the competence to do a job. But to excel as a leader, you also need to expand your perspective and ensure you have proper motives.

When your leadership is universal, you have met your goal. Meaning, you can serve anywhere. You recognize that your role is to take care of your people, regardless of their role in the organization. Here are some real-world examples of what I mean:

A CEO knows the responsibilities and goals for each department operating within his budget, but he does not need to understand how every dollar and cent is being used. A financial overview is essential. Staying in the black is a requirement. But overall, the goal is to understand how to lead the people responsible and accountable for each of those areas.

Consider the role of those who have served as Chief of Staff of the U.S. Air Force. They are the four-star general in charge of the entire Air Force. They probably have never completed an acquisition request. They have probably never run the logistics function of a personnel deployment function where the military ensures each deployer has their required items. They lead many subject matter experts. How? Because the Chief of Staff understands the mindset and heartset the military needs to be successful. They know what the mission is and how to do it most effectively. They focus on ensuring the people are organized, trained, and equipped for war. They focus on providing the tools airmen and guardians need to succeed.

When you are an administrator, you cannot be hyperfocused on developing your tool and skillsets. If you are the CEO of McDonalds, you do not worry about how quickly you personally can turn a hamburger; you focus on enabling the people whose job it is to develop more efficient processes. Do not mistake the thought here to be that a leader does not have to have a clear understanding of their work environment or the tasks required of their people. You must be able to communicate about employees' pain points and understand their vocabulary when presented with areas for improvement. Learn the basics; but, as a leader, focus on leading your people. Unless your leadership role requires a very technical specialty (e.g., supervising pediatric heart surgery at a trauma center), you should be able to be universal in your placement in leadership roles. You should be just as effective at running a Levi's factory as you are at leading a rental car company.

COMMIT TO PERSONAL PRINCIPLES

CHAPTER 8

LEADERS CONVEY VALUE WHEN...

THEY DEVELOP FOUNDATIONAL PRINCIPLES THAT GOVERN THEIR DECISION-MAKING.

8. COMMIT TO PERSONAL PRINCIPLES

Now that we have gone over the four elements that make a good leader, it is time to take a personal assessment. Ask yourself, "What is important to me? What principles am I not willing to compromise?" You must know who you are before you can lead others.

"With integrity nothing else counts. Without integrity nothing else counts."
— Hindu Proverb

Listed below are five principles I set up for my own personal assessment. Yours might look different from mine, and that is okay. If you do not have your own, feel free to take mine and use them until you determine yours. As you read them, I challenge you to explore which is a fit for you, and which you would replace with something else.

Represent What Matters Most

Even though the culture of a workplace is bigger than you, it should not violate your core principles. Personal principles represent you. While we cannot push our principles on anyone else, we can create a culture which respects those principles.

As a Christian, representing Jesus Christ matters to me. It defines who I am and what I do, and the rationale for my personal and interpersonal conduct is wrapped up in this principle. To others, the most important value is to represent their family name, so they will focus on making their parents proud. Some desire to succeed because they want to leave a legacy of hard work. We each have values and should aim to consistently represent them.

When you make a decision, your principles will stand strong and direct you. You should stack every decision against your principles to make sure it does not violate the culture you want to build.

Lead by Example

In his book *Words and Deeds*, Charles Causey says, "To have integrity means to have an absence of duplicity....A man of integrity has his words and deeds integrated, with no sunlight between the two."[5]

Leading by example is only possible when you first clearly define your principles and what you stand for. Demonstrating a strong work ethic and showing empathy and kindness to others are standard behaviors a leader should model. As the leader, you must model the behaviors and attitudes that you want to see in others. Setting high standards for yourself will make it easier to expect your team to adopt similar standards.

Consistency and authenticity are required to prevent a "say-do gap"—the distance between what we say and what we do. We can have all the right principles lined up, but inconsistency breeds distrust and disrespect, and that is a hard mountain to win back. The commander referenced in chapter 2 who wore her uniform sloppily will be hard-pressed to get her unit to wear their uniforms crisply and correctly because despite any comment she makes, she does not illustrate that appearance actually matters to her.

> *"Integrity...is measured by the distance between your lips and your life."*[6]
> — Mark Sanborn in *You Don't Need a Title to Be a Leader*

As a leader, you cannot expect your team to show up on time if you are not making that a priority. If you arrive late every day and miss deadlines, then people will not take timelines seriously. If you turn in an assignment late twice, they think they can turn it in late every time because you are the standard. What we do in moderation people will allow in excess, so we must be careful with what we allow and do not allow; what we communicate, when, and how.

> *"Leading by example is the most powerful advice you can give to anybody."*[7]
> — N. R. Narayana Murthy

---

5   (Causey 2018)
6   (Sanborn 2006)
7   (Murthy, n.d.)

If you have a group project, everyone works on the group project. If a person finishes their task early, set them up with the next. Show that the job is not finished until everyone finishes. Actively dive in and help; people appreciate a leader who doesn't just direct but works, too.

When your team is planning for an event, be active in discussions. Give input and feedback, then offer your help wherever needed. Be willing to take on tasks that are outside your normal responsibilities if it helps the team achieve its goals. This participation is particularly important during demanding work seasons or special circumstances like audits. It's encouraging for your team when they see you in the yoke pulling with them instead of leading from the side. Their commitment to the team and business feeds off your own.

Be a Servant Leader

"Help your brother's boat across and your own will reach the shore."
— Hindu Proverb

Servant leadership means prioritizing the needs of others before our own. It means leading by serving, rather than expecting others to serve us. Nothing is beneath us, and we don't ask anyone to do what we are not willing to do ourselves.

If you are hosting an event at the office, don't just head home after the event ends. Stay and help clean up. Be one of the last to leave. When you pitch in and show that nothing is too small for you, your team will respect that far more than any title or position.

This ideal goes hand in hand with leading by example. I once had a boss who struggled to be a servant leader. The building where we worked had a faulty fire system and the fire alarm would trip often, requiring us to leave until security cleared the building. The false alarms grew tedious.

One winter morning, the alarm sounded and there we were, standing in twenty-degree weather without our coats, because we evacuated quickly, per the instructions she had provided across staff meetings. As we waited for the all clear, I noticed my boss in her office, typing away, enjoying the warmth while the rest of us froze outside.

My respect for my boss was taxed before that moment, but when I saw her in that office, ignoring the alarm while expecting the rest of us to obey, all respect evaporated. A servant leader would have been out in that cold with us, obeying the same rules as the rest of us. If your team must endure, endure with them.

If we go a little deeper, we'll see that serving others involves intentionality. It requires actively listening to our team's needs, showing empathy and compassion, and taking action to help them achieve their goals. By putting the needs of our team first, we can build strong relationships and foster a sense of community that will ultimately lead to greater success. Out of respect, your team will want to prove their own reliability through hard work and dedication.

"Caring is the ultimate team-building strategy."[8]
— Jon Gordon and Mike Smith in *You Win in the Locker Room First*

Be a Customized Leader

A good leader will tailor communication and encouragement to fit the individual needs of each colleague. Maybe you have an employee who never responds to email but does well with verbal communication. Or maybe an employee is a better follower than an idea generator. Being a customized leader takes time and mental energy, but the effort makes us more effective as leaders and provides great value to the team. It is important to recognize that not everybody responds the same to affection, correction, and direction. People need different things at different times. Guidelines are smart to have, but not every situation should be textbook.

As a leader, I worked with a colleague who was an excellent doer. He could accomplish every task he received at a high level. He was very efficient and took copious notes on every task I asked him to complete. He was advanced into a prominent leadership role in the organization and I expected that he would naturally and quickly transition from doing to leading (although at the time, neither I nor anyone else had explained the difference between the two). I told him he was accountable for a monthly status brief on programs and personnel. My only requirements beyond the information requirement was that I wanted the content delivery standardized in appearance and to look professional.

I was surprised when I sat down and received the first brief. The presentation

---

8   (Gordon 2015)

slideshow did not meet my expectations. It was not professional as the fonts were different sizes and there was no continuity of content. To be fair, he had compiled the information from various team members, so he took their data and just copied it directly into the slideshow. I was disappointed, and frustrated, but I did not want to overreact, so I simply tried to correct the situation. I defined a font and font size, and outlined a clear template for him to follow for the next brief. I felt accomplished because I was a "good leader." Instead of diminishing the poor presentation, I responded by doing the "hard work" of thinking through a template that could be used and reused. I had successfully made the process simpler for him.

Later that same day, he asked for some time to speak. He was upset because he felt that I was micromanaging his work and that I was trying to oversee the smallest details of his workload, down to the font size he used. It took me time to understand where I had failed because I thought I was helping him.

I neglected a couple of areas here. First, I did not provide expectation management. My expectation was that he understood the difference between being accountable and being responsible. Practically, I expected that if he received products that were improperly formatted he would return them to the sender or fix them himself prior to utilizing the products. Second, I expected him to understand that showing nonstandardized presentations to senior leaders would not present a professional appearance. Overall, I should have had a teaching mindset as opposed to a corrective mindset. I neglected to teach him the standard expectations at his new level. Also, I failed to convey that when I chose a font it was to simplify the process. It was something he did not have to worry about and instead, he could focus on the presentation's content. I neglected to understand him as a person. I failed to lead him and serve him in the way he needed. I failed to exercise customized leadership.

Although this example seems very small in impact, it had a huge impact because he needed direction, but I was providing correction. And since we were relatively new to working together, I had not laid the foundation of affection. It is difficult to receive correction without having an assurance of affection. Remember the quote often attributed to Teddy Roosevelt, "Nobody cares how much you know until they know how much you care." A good ratio I follow is that people need 70% affection, 20% direction, and 10% correction. I should have pulled him aside after the meeting and said, "I appreciate how much work you put into this. Overall, I have the information I need, but I want to set you up for success. I will hold you accountable for the overall presentation, and that presentation is not standardized. A standardized presentation is expected and shows order. A font I have seen used regularly is Times New Roman, size 12. I recommend using it across the entirety of future presentations." At that point, we could have had a discussion about any questions, about the overall approach to when senior leaders request a brief, and various other topics.

If you need help expanding this ability, there are countless resources available that provide insight into team members' working and learning styles. Personality tests, group activities, and retreats all lend to this endeavor and are great investments.

Don't Be a Jerk

There is nothing complex about this concept. We all inherently know what the "jerkiest" thing is in given situations. Choose not to do it.

These five principles will help you have an inviolable foundation. I recommend that you establish them and then commit to never breaking them. They will help you keep your integrity.

In addition, here are some general guidelines to keep yourself out of trouble. These guidelines serve as a filter to determine whether or not you should immediately reverse course and/or change your environment. The first four guidelines focus on the relationship between you and your environment, and the fifth guideline focuses on you alone.

1. Don't Do Anything Dumb, Different, or Dangerous

Your opportunity to serve as a leader is dependent on your personal ability to sustain the character and conduct that earned you the opportunity in the first place. People watch you, and your consistency will allow you to retain trust.

2. Sleep in Your Own Bed with Your Own Spouse

Have enough presence of mind to be capable of going home. Do not allow yourself to be in a compromising position because you did not have the wherewithal to leave. Clear boundaries will ensure propriety.

3. Spend Your Own Money

Misappropriation of funds or misuse of funds are both reasons why people become disqualified from positions. Keep a strict line between company resources and personal resources.

4. Nothing Good Happens at Events after 9:30 PM

As a leader, people want to know that you care enough to attend activities outside of work; but they do not want their supervisor to hang around while they are enjoying their down time. I recommend going to events, saying hello to everyone, and then leaving after an hour.

5. Remember That "Rest" Is an Active Verb

Sometimes we treat the tasks in every area of our lives as if they are glass balls. We juggle our schedules and activities, striving to accomplish everything as if it's all precious. The risk then is the glass shatters, leaving us responsible for the consequences.

A lifestyle that treats every action as precious glass requires a great level of effort, energy, intensity, and focus. It is helpful for a short time, but not sustainable. During a time where I overtaxed myself by working long hours in every area, I suffered significant burn out and my mind and body could barely function. I found myself unable to complete normal tasks in a timely manner and I was exhausted, but I could not sleep because I was busy thinking of the items on my to-do list. I was at risk for making poor decisions in every area of my life.

I realized two important facts during that time. One was that I must continuously reclassify which balls are glass balls in my life. If I am working on a large project, today that might be a glass ball, but tomorrow it may not be. Tomorrow, my family may be the glass ball on which I need to focus, and I may need to make several check-in calls, or schedule time with them so we can connect. Every day as I look at my schedule, and the needs of those around me, I can restructure my priorities to ensure the true glass balls don't get dropped.

The other important realization for me was that rest is an active verb. Sometimes sitting and doing nothing is the most helpful thing I can do. Refreshing occurs when I actively stop and seek to transition out of the noisy environment. Rest should not include your smartphone or making any task lists. It doesn't have to specifically mean sleep, but you do have to remove yourself from the chaos and allow yourself a realistic time frame to regenerate. Stop thinking about your requirements. It will be hard at first, but I promise you, being disciplined about rest will allow you to be more effective at serving.

I know we have covered a lot in this section regarding how to keep from becoming distracted as a leader. These are the principles that help to guide my conduct so that I can be the leader people want to follow. As Roy Disney said, "It's not hard to make decisions when you know what your values are."[9] I want to follow somebody who has good moral character, who is consistent with what they say and do, and who understands that I am not simply a pawn for their advancement. I want to follow someone who wants to build a team and who is willing to take the time and effort to learn about my skills and knowledge. I definitely do not want to work for a jerk. When you consider personal principles, think about the type of leader you naturally gravitate toward and the characteristics you admire. Most likely, those are your core principles, too.

---

9 (Hung 2021, quoting Roy Disney)

LEADING OTHERS

PROVIDE CLEAR DIRECTION

CHAPTER 9

LEADERS CONVEY VALUE WHEN...

THEY COMMUNICATE THE TEAM'S VISION, MISSION, AND GOALS.

9. PROVIDE CLEAR DIRECTION

Leaders navigate the ship. They set the course and provide the "why" behind every move. If the leader falters or fails to make the reasoning for the course clear, it will be difficult to train aspiring leaders to make wise choices on behalf of the business.

There are three foundational elements that a company should establish and articulate:

Vision

Our vision is why we do what we do. Where do you want to be in twenty years? What do you want to be known for? What is the legacy you want to leave? Consider those things when conceptualizing a vision for your company.

Example: "To be the premier construction company in the northwest Indiana region, known for our commitment to excellence, innovative solutions, and to provide safe, good-paying jobs for skilled workers."

Mission

Our mission is what we must do every day to accomplish our vision. A mission is the vehicle that drives us to our vision, and this statement conveys what activities must take place in order to realize the vision. If our vision is to be the best in the Midwest, then we will define our focus. We can measure that through revenue generation or customer satisfaction. However, our mission and vision must align.

Example: "At XYZ Construction, our mission is to deliver superior construction services with integrity and dedication. Through collaboration, craftsmanship, and cutting-edge technology, we strive to exceed client expectations and foster a safe environment for our employees as they develop their practical skills."

As you can see, XYZ Construction intends to meet their vision of "best" through the lens of customer satisfaction.

Goals

Goals are the incremental action items completed each day to fulfill our mission. Start with the big picture of where you want to be in twenty years and work backward. Many people get started without setting long-term goals and that wastes time, money, and resources. If your vision is to be the best XYZ in the Midwest, as measured by customer satisfaction, it is wise to center your goals around that. Goals help you focus on what serves your mission, which in turn, serves your vision.

Example of Fiscal Year Goals:
- Client Satisfaction: Achieve a client satisfaction rate of 95% or higher as measured through customer response forms, through exceptional project delivery, responsive communication, and personalized service.
- Safety: Maintain a zero-accident safety record, promoting a culture of safety throughout the organization.
- Employee Development: Send each department head to one additional training or professional development opportunity to ensure their growth within the company.
- Financial Stability and Growth: Maintain a strong financial position through prudent fiscal management and strategic bidding with the aim of expanding our footprint in the region and maintaining a starting pay of $25 per hour to our employees.

If you don't have an articulated vision, mission statement, and goals, utilize your team to establish them. Their input will create buy-in and serve as another guide to keep the business on the right track as it grows.

When team members have clarity on the direction and standards of the company, they experience job stability and can further develop their decision-making capability. Often, employees won't offer suggestions or criticisms because they are concerned about making the wrong decision. If they know the filters by which decisions are made, they will feel more comfortable acting in that role because they are familiar with how the leader processes opportunities.

Every decision should be predicated on the vision of your business. If you have a great business opportunity, test it against your vision. Does it align with your mission? If you are setting up your budget, does each department line up with where you are headed? Aligning every decision with your company's vision, mission, and goals will keep you on the right path.

PART III
LEADING OTHERS

LEADING OTHERS

IDENTIFY POTENTIAL AND PROMOTE APPROPRIATELY

CHAPTER 10

LEADERS CONVEY VALUE WHEN...

THEY PROMOTE THE RIGHT LEADERS AND PROPERLY REWARD HIGH ACHIEVERS.

10. IDENTIFY POTENTIAL AND PROMOTE APPROPRIATELY

In Jim Collins' book *Good to Great*, he introduces the concept of putting the right people on the bus in the right seats. This metaphor recognizes that an organization needs people who exhibit different skills to fill the multi-faceted needs of a business. Leaders are the ones who recognize the skills and put people in the bus where they will thrive—for the sake of both the teammate and the organization.

Identify Potential Leaders

I want leaders in my organization to understand that both the need for leadership, and the weight of the responsibility are very real. In the military, when you take command, you raise your right hand and say, "Ma'am, I assume command." You own the role as a leader. Leadership is something you assume but cannot discard.

I remember the first day I took command: I was walking into my unit alongside a senior leader I trusted and respected. I had a theory about where I wanted to put my office, and I had some other small decisions I was contemplating. It was funny—I was sure about my ability to lead during the interview selection process for the role, but as soon as I received my orders to assume command, I was immediately unsure of the simple decisions. I asked my colleague his opinion and he said, "You're the commander, ma'am." I paused, thought about it, and figured his words were intended to say he did not have a true opinion or recommendation, and the choice would be up to me. I rephrased the question and asked for his opinion again. He said, "Whatever you decide ma'am; you're the commander." I changed the subject, and we came to another point in the conversation where I wanted his opinion. Again, he said, "Ma'am, you're the commander." I read his stoic approach as a seeming unwillingness to help me make decisions, which was counter to his normal behavior. I realized then that he was actively seeking to help me own my role. I could not start off with a crutch—I had to be confident that I was responsible for my role. I was the only one accountable for organizing, training, and equipping this unit for war.

I needed to own that responsibility, and part of that was knowing that the decision-making rested with me. Then, and only then, could I ask for assistance. I could not abdicate decision-making because I was scared or unnerved. I was the leader and I needed to own it.

When you stop owning that you are accountable for the results, when it stops mattering, that's when mistakes are made. In the profession of arms, when leaders fail to lead, people die. We must seek leaders who understand that their role requires an intentional assumption of the weight of their role.

Having critical thinking and problem-solving skills, accountability, teachability, a bent toward taking initiative, and the ability to work well with others are some helpful mindsets and heartsets to look for when trying to identify future leaders. Lee Iacocca once said, "I hire people brighter than me and then I get out of their way."[10] He understood that the future of his organization depended on identifying strong leaders.

While personality tests can be helpful to find potential leaders, observing behavior and performance is also crucial. Determine how well a person works both under pressure and with seemingly insignificant tasks. Do the others respond well to this person? If colleagues respect them, it speaks well of behavior exhibited when the boss is not around.

"A team is only as good as the members that comprise it.
Therefore, strong leaders are aware that who they select to be on the team and part of
the organization they lead is critical and must be thoughtfully accomplished."[11]
— Daniel York in *The Strong Leader's Hand: Teamwork*

If you are not directly involved in the hiring process, challenge human resources personnel to consider qualified individuals for the level of leadership required. You should be as intimately involved in this process as possible.

As we have discussed, just because someone knows what they are doing does not mean they are qualified to lead. Recognize that it is nice to find someone who knows the industry, but if you prioritize that above their ability to lead a team, you will have a situation where people will fail to thrive. If the person you desire to hire does not know how to lead, ensure they are willing to learn.

---

10   (Iacocca and Novak 1984)
11   (York 2017)

"When you hire good people, and you provide good jobs and good wages and a career, good things are going to happen."[12]
— Jim Sinegal

Resist Assembling an Echo Chamber

While it might be comfortable to surround yourself with a team that fits the same mold as you, that practice leads to the development of an echo chamber. Business and personal growth is found when team members respectfully challenge the status quo. Therefore, it is a best practice to intentionally diversify your leadership in background, education, strength, and culture. Find the diamonds in the rough and develop them. You should not have only "yes men" who parrot what they perceive you want to hear. Humble leaders who actively encourage sharing differing opinions have a better chance of seeing the full picture.

For most of my professional career, I have been a "unicorn" leader: my appearance, my background, my culture, and my perspective all differ from those that I work with. Even my hobbies, TV shows, and food from my Black/Filipino heritage are different from most of the other people who sit in the room with me. Throughout my career, I have appreciated the leaders who gave me the opportunity to prove that my differences meant I brought a unique viewpoint to the table.

I understand this example wades into current social and cultural issues, but this perspective may help some leaders who have not had the opportunity to talk to someone openly about this issue. Because of the recent cultural emphasis on diversity, equity, and inclusion (DEI) (which is necessary, but requires proper execution), people assume that promoting a minority woman to upper ranks is a handout to meet quotas. In the military, I have not seen promotions for minorities simply because they are minorities, to be the case. In the upper levels of the military, the reality is that people's lives are on the line, and no senior leader I know would authorize an incompetent non-leader to assume command for the sake of filling some sort of DEI quota. The gravity of the responsibility of leadership demands that leaders are thoroughly prepared to lead.

Often, I feel the pressure of working twice as hard to get a seat at the administrative table, only to feel I have to prove I had the skills again once I am there.

---

12   (Ruggeri 2009)

I say this not to conjure up emotion, but to point out that there are unfortunate stigmas that some people must overcome. I have even heard micro-aggressive statements like, "You're more articulate than I thought you would be," or seen people be visibly taken aback when they learn I am the one in charge during a meeting. While it may be unintentional, it is a frustration to be dealt with every single day. If you are trying to intentionally avoid the echo chamber, this explanation may help you understand the pain points of new leaders who are different races or genders, or who have different work experience or education than is typical in your industry.

Recognize That Promotions Are Not the Only Reward

I spoke at an event where a Chief Information Officer (CIO) presented a dilemma he faced at work. One of the man's team members was skilled in running cables and setting up networks, and had proven to be reliable and forward-thinking. Because of his performance and reputation, the team member was promoted to oversee all the networking teams. The problem? The new leader was absolutely miserable in his new role. He felt incredibly insecure leading people and not managing projects directly. The CIO lamented that he spent 80% of his days collaborating with this struggling manager to solve the day's issues. His question concerned how to fix this situation.

My first question to him was whether or not the employee wanted this new position. He shared that the new role was a reward and upper management wanted to acknowledge how hard this man worked, and show appreciation for how he had grown so incredibly competent at his craft. This was a promotion, and they felt he was the best candidate for the job. Here is the problem. The employee may be the best at their job, but that doesn't make them a proper candidate for leadership. When leaders promote someone who does not fit well in a role, it results in low morale, decreased productivity, and even mistakes. The team suffers, and they feel less than rewarded.

To prevent this mishap, ask people how they want to be rewarded. Consider a private versus a public show of appreciation. Perhaps they want a financial incentive, the opportunity to assist on a prime project, public recognition in the company newsletter or social media, or even time off. A reward becomes impactful the more the awardee desires it.

Move Insufficient Leaders

Often, companies promote because they have limited options. Have you ever worked in a situation where the boss was clearly in over his head or had such a toxic personality that people dreaded working at the company? Those types of people are maxed beyond their capabilities, but remain in place because nobody wants to fire anybody.

Ill-advised promotions that do not help the team or build trust and confidence of team members must be addressed by a leader. Strategic moves are not usually "fun," especially when it involves having difficult conversations and making tough calls. However, leadership requires strength and sensitivity. Letting someone go isn't the only option; perhaps there is a role elsewhere in the company that is a better fit. Remember, if you aren't putting the right person in the right seat, you keep that person from finding their best fit—and that hurts both the individual and the team.

DEVELOP OTHER LEADERS

CHAPTER 11

LEADERS CONVEY VALUE WHEN...

THEY ACTIVELY MENTOR AND INVEST IN FUTURE LEADERS.

11. DEVELOP OTHER LEADERS.

There is a belief among some leaders that if they are the only person who can do their job, no one can replace them. Those leaders are the least effective for the same reason. Not to be morbid, but if they get hit by a bus, how worthwhile was it that they were the only one who knew what they knew? It is important to transfer both knowledge and experiential learning.

Our colleagues must have an environment where they get to practice leading without the pressure and accountability of leadership. It is the best place to be. They learn and train until they can find stability and security for themselves.

I continually see this illustration of developing others as a pilot. I remember the fear and trepidation I felt the first time I ever sat in a cockpit. Looking over at my instructor, I thought, "I hope this guy wants to live because if he doesn't, I do not have enough skills to keep us alive." Now that I am an instructor, I tell my students, "Don't worry until I worry. I will make sure that we get home safely."

Over time, my instructor made fewer corrections and offered fewer affirmations. Then one day I realized I knew where I was going, I knew what I was doing, and I was the one planning the flight. The instructor had done his job, and I was ready.

I started flying with friends just for entertainment because I had developed a comfort level. I knew I could perform at the level required of me because my instructor had trained me appropriately. As a flight instructor, when I allow a student to fly solo for the first time, it is because they feel that confidence and I feel that confidence in them, too.

In my unit, we have what is called a "continuity binder," a designated place to store all the technical and tactical information to make sure that we are not reinventing the wheel every time a situation arises. The situations and events we deal with are largely the same, but the context changes.

In the same way we are prepared for the actual work to have a line of continuity, leaders must focus on providing a continuity of vision. You need to have people who can come in and take your position if you are unable to serve any longer. They must understand, and be able to accomplish the team's vision, and know how to build the people who will accomplish the mission.

Don't think of developing other leaders as "working yourself out of a job." Rather, it is having the confidence that whatever life may throw your way, the mission will go on and there's someone competent to take care of your people. When you invest in your people and it is time for them to step up, they will enter their new role confident in their capabilities and in the vision itself.

Developing other leaders may seem like a daunting task, but it doesn't have to be. Here are seven ways to grow future leaders:

Provide Opportunities for Growth

Once you have someone in mind who you would like to mentor, start providing opportunities to develop their skills. This could involve delegating more difficult tasks to team members or allowing them to lead meetings or presentations. You can provide professional development opportunities, such as training or mentorship programs. Think about what you do in your position and have your protégé practice each duty.

Coaching your mentee as they practice will help you not only gradually build their confidence and skills, but free up your time to focus on other priorities. It is important to note that many leaders avoid training others because they feel they are too busy. If that is your thought process, change it! You are too busy not to train a leader. Bring them along with you, proverbially and physically, as you are participating in activities you normally do. If the two of you are in the same meeting, focus on finding opportunities there.

There is an old story of two people discussing training. The manager who is too busy to train says, "What if we train them and they leave?" The leader says, "What if we don't train them and they stay?" An investment of your time today will reap a multitude of benefits later.

Promote Learning

When you want your people to succeed and reach their potential, you will do what it takes to get them there. Encourage learning and development by providing resources and opportunities for growth. This can include books, online courses, conferences, and workshops.

There are in-house training sessions and team-building retreats that teach team members how to learn from each other and work together more effectively. But remember, a leader who is a team player won't just send their team, they will attend with them and take part in the activities.

When they return from these events, have them provide a short overview of the major points they learned. He who does the teaching does the learning. This will not only solidify the principles gained throughout the training, but could encourage others to engage in opportunities as their interest is piqued.

Give Feedback

> *"Feedback is the breakfast of champions."*[13]
> — Ken Blanchard

Feedback provides potential leaders with the chance to improve their skills. Often, before providing my opinion, I say, "How do you think it went?" This allows me to hear their recap of the event. Oftentimes, I find people are harder on themselves than I ever would have been. Asking this question allows me to pinpoint their focal points. For example, if I am assisting someone with public speaking, and their perception of their most recent speaking opportunity is that they went over time, and that was the most pressing difficulty, I would know that they believe that is one of the top priorities for a public speaker. I agree with that sentiment, but would provide feedback on content, audience engagement, eye contact, and volume as well. Be specific about what they did well and where they can improve, but speak in an affirming way. You don't want to shield them from the results of bad decisions, and this is the time to walk them through how to handle consequences when they happen.

Also, encourage them to take on new challenges, especially in areas where they struggle. We all have our weaknesses. Instead of simply pointing them out, encourage them to use failure as a catalyst to further growth in those areas. Of course, provide support as needed and make yourself available for conversation.

---

13   (Blanchard 2009)

Encourage Collaboration

You should not underestimate the importance of building relationships with your team. Spend time and energy on building a positive, supportive relationship with your up-and-coming leaders.

Lead by example in this area. Take them into meetings, have them sit in on discussions with team leaders and individual members. Then, encourage them to do collaborations of their own. These are skills that will aid them greatly when they oversee their own team.

Recognize and Reward

Go beyond merely providing standard feedback and affirmations. Remember, you are mentoring a leader who will one day do what you do. They will carry the load you carry and bear the responsibility of the position on their shoulders.

Rewarding their efforts, whether publicly or privately, strengthens their confidence and encourages their endeavors. Whether you choose public recognition, promotions, or bonuses, celebrating their success encourages them to continue to develop their skills.

Be Available

While I was at Air Command and Staff College, the U.S. Air Force's intermediate developmental education program, one of my assignments was to interview a senior leader and discuss how they overcame a difficulty during their command time. This meeting was designed to allow me to ask questions, learn about their perspectives, and write my reflections to share with my classmates.

As a Black woman in the military, I wanted to connect with a leader who had experiences I could relate to, so I reached out to General Dana Nelson, a female Black general who has shattered the proverbial glass ceiling many times over.

When I asked for her time, she was more than willing to set up a meeting with me. In fact, she was very familiar with our interview assignment—she had completed this exercise with several others prior to our meeting.

Not only did General Nelson make time for that one conversation, but she has taken my calls many times since. Whether I needed mentorship, a review of my performance reports, or a group speaker, she always said yes. It was so refreshing to engage with a leader willing to help those who probably could not offer her anything in return. Her example challenged me to extend the same courtesy to my subordinates.

When a leader makes themselves available for one-on-one conversations and mentorship, it can set forth a growth trajectory that far surpasses anything one might learn in a classroom setting. It is a great way to develop the heartset and mindset in a team member.

Inspire Others

I am a Tuskegee Airman-inspired pilot. These determined, dedicated, and highly qualified airmen were the first Black Americans to fly for the military during World War II. They held the record for having one of the lowest loss records of all escort fighter groups, and were in constant demand by Allied bomber units for their unmatched record and skill in the air.

As distinguished as the Tuskegee Airmen were, they still struggled with racism both in America and among their colleagues overseas. Instead of returning home after the war and saying, "I quit," they stayed and became leaders, continuing to promote in the military. They were amazing men, fighting through adversity and emerging victorious on the other side.

In commemoration of these incredible airmen, there's an inscription on a statue in the Honor Court at the U.S. Air Force Academy that says, "They rose from adversity through competence, courage, commitment, and capacity to serve America on silver wings and to set a standard few will transcend."

As a junior at the Academy, I had the privilege of participating in an event honoring the Tuskegee Airmen. I was incredibly honored to connect with Lt. Col. Lee Archer, the first person of African American descent to shoot down five enemy aircraft. He was the first Black ace!

Determined to get his autograph, I introduced myself. He took time to talk with me and asked about my classes, my major, and what I planned to do after graduation. I told him I was approved for pilot training but intended to pursue intelligence instead. I had set my heart on becoming an ambassador—or higher—and knew intelligence was the path forward.

What he said next changed my life forever. He asked, "If you don't stand on our shoulders, who will?"

The conviction in that thought moved me. These men fought for acceptance, fought for the chance to fly, fought to overcome stigmas and performed well above the standard. They made their shoulders broad enough for so many others to stand on, and here I was, at the Air Force Academy, the premier pilot producing institution, and I had never considered learning how to fly.

His words captured my attention, and it was at that moment that I decided to fly. After I earned my license, I discovered there were fewer than 150 African American female professional pilots in the United States. I received a lot of attention for being a pilot; however, I saw the statistic not as a matter of pride, but rather as a reality I wanted to change. I did not want to merely be an anomaly, praised for being one of the few. Rather, I wanted to inspire others to stand on my shoulders, just as Lt. Col. Archer did. I shared my thoughts with my colleague, Captain Chris Campbell, and he articulated the concept far better than I could. He said, "There's no point in blazing a trail if the trail doesn't become a road."[14]

That's the type of leader I want to become. I don't want it to be about me blazing a trail, but about those coming behind me. I want to think long-term and I want people to have a road that is built for their travel. I want others to stand on my shoulders.

---

14   (Campbell, n.d.)

PROVIDE EXPECTATION MANAGEMENT

CHAPTER 12

LEADERS CONVEY VALUE WHEN...

THEY SET CLEAR EXPECTATIONS AND DELEGATE APPROPRIATELY.

12. PROVIDE EXPECTATION MANAGEMENT

There are some things I prefer to be done in a certain way; but largely, I encourage my people to make decisions without me. After all, I would much rather have to slow someone down than push them to do things.

If I am doing a good job communicating clearly, then my team knows the thought process behind how we can best execute our mission. I do not just want to teach people what to think. I want to teach them how to think. Teaching people what to think ensures they know my thoughts on certain topics. It is useful when I prefer items to be done a certain way. However, teaching people how to think allows them to see the rationale behind why we do things the way we do. This allows them to grow more comfortable with decision-making, minimize delays and frustration on both ends, and streamline processes to aid in the personal development of the team.

I once introduced a new second-in-command to my team. He was a driven, disciplined individual, but lacked the confidence to move forward without checking with me every few minutes. I took time to teach him the protocol I expected in most common situations, and within a few months he became much more comfortable answering the question, "What would she want in this situation?" While there was an initial time investment with my new team member, the successful result was that it ultimately took much off my plate.

Here are some practical things I have found that work well in providing expectation management:

Provide Context for How You View Issues

"The sky is falling!" How many times has someone come into the office to present an issue that must be dealt with immediately? When building leaders, one of the most helpful things to do is to provide proper context. When people bring issues to our attention, recognize that people can have a tendency to elevate issues because they have a limited scope. When the time and place are appropriate, we have a responsiblity to help our team understand which issues are mountains (difficult to overcome) and which are molehills (easily overcome).

Then, together we can deal with the issue accordingly.

To help determine which issues are mountains and which are molehills, I developed the standard that mountains occur when something is on fire and people are shooting at us. If the issue does not fall into either of those categories, it is most likely not a mountain of an issue. Determining ahead of time which things will cause you to be in emergency management mode will allow you to respond to issues as opposed to reacting to them. Talk your teammates through the situation or ask questions to shed light on the situation and help them see the problem as it really is.

Addressing problems logically and thoughtfully is an excellent way to lead by example, and can help teach your team how to appropriately respond to issues.

Direct Concerns through the Appropriate Channels

Sometimes leaders think they must be the ones to field all the questions and problems within their business, but this is not effective leadership. Not only could they better spend their time elsewhere, they cause their future leaders' growth to be stunted.

Do not solve problems that are not required to be solved at your level. Once, I worked in mid-level management, and in our organization we had a commander who was so adept at problem solving and was so well-respected with a wide network that our problems were solved quickly. It became easy for us to bring her all of our concerns.

One day, I brought her a problem and she redirected me to ask her second-in-command to solve that problem because he was my direct supervisor. Honestly, I was a bit annoyed because I knew that it would be a longer process to get help that she could have provided immediately.

As I matured in my leadership, I realized that her second-in-command probably felt left out of the discussion. He did not know what his immediate subordinates needed. He did not know how we tried to problem-solve. He did not get to grow his network by connecting about issues. She was taking opportunities from him.

As a leader, when you encounter someone who foregoes the proper channels, simply redirect them with, "Did you ask [your supervisor] about this?"

Set Clear Expectations and Encourage Questions

I want leaders in my organization to grow in the confidence of their decision-making. I tell them that when they make a decision, I will respond in one of three ways: "Good job!"; "Can we reverse that decision?"; or, "Next time, I'd like to be involved in that."

There is no scolding or animosity in my answers, because I want to encourage them to make decisions. If I scold their decision because I would have done it differently, then I am shutting them down, increasing their "decision paralysis," and ultimately making more work for myself, because they will stop making decisions, and develop an overreliance on me to make them.

When I calmly and carefully communicate my preferences, I am giving them another tool to help make future decisions. Over time, we will align so well that I will hardly have to change anything. It is a beautiful process that takes effort, but is well worth it.

Part of that education process is letting them ask questions. As they ask questions, I try to say, "I trust your judgment," if the matter of concern is something for which I do not have a strong preference, and whatever they decide will be fine. If I have a clear preference, I will be direct and say, "I prefer we handle it in this way." Not only does this encourage their willingness to make a decision, it also defines in which areas they can freely operate to make decisions.

Sometimes dog owners use electric fences to keep their pets safe in the yard. The dogs test the boundaries to know their perimeters, and once they learn them, they are content in their allotted area and run about freely. But if they hit the fence, they know to adjust their course. While this might not be the best analogy, the same idea applies to allowing our team to explore their boundaries.

Additionally, when communicating expectations, aim to eliminate as many tactical unknowns as possible. This does not mean find every solution to every problem or answer every question in the problem set before delegating a task to someone. It simply means contextualizing the task. Some info you should provide includes:

- Key information about the task
- The clear questions to which you need answers
- The format and time you want to receive the information

After sharing that information, I like to follow up with a time statement. "Overall, this should take you about ten minutes, and if you're spending more than ten minutes on it, then you're probably doing more than I need you to do." I base the timeline on various factors including their skillset, the ability of the resources required to complete the task, the number of uncontrollable items within the task (think about if there will be a need to coordinate with other people's schedules) and other elements. Overall, I want people to know the reality of my expectations. I have asked this question, as a subordinate, to my leadership, and it has saved me time and energy. Sometimes I realized I was thinking too deeply into a project, when in reality, all my boss needed was a surface-level answer to their question.

I try to set my people up for success by having honest conversations from the start and asking their opinions as they acclimate. The more your people test their decision-making opportunities, the more they learn how to think critically and to practically explore areas where they can grow their skills. This allows them to train in their heartset, mindset, skillset, and toolset.

LEADING OTHERS

DEVELOP TWO-WAY CONFIDENCE

CHAPTER 13

LEADERS CONVEY VALUE WHEN...

THEY GIVE NEW LEADERS
THE CONFIDENCE TO GROW.

13. DEVELOP TWO-WAY CONFIDENCE

Remember that phrase, "No one cares how much you know until they know how much you care?" When our people feel loved, heard, and encouraged, they will be more receptive to constructive criticism and opportunities for growth.

Here are three phrases I use when I want to develop two-way confidence in my team:

"I trust your judgment."

I say this often because I want people to know I believe it. And I do believe it because I have put in the time to teach them how to think. We have collaborated on what sound decision-making looks like.

When we have a great working relationship, I don't have to manage every decision every day. I have the freedom to focus on only the things that I can do, which furthers the business and my colleagues, as both have the optimal opportunity to grow.

"I want to set you up for success."

If I have a teammate working toward a goal or promotion, I will be very clear with my expectations for them to earn an opportunity to excel. I had a colleague who wanted to be promoted, but I needed to see how he provided critical thought and analysis to our group decisions. I said, "I know you want a promotion. What I need to see from you is how you think critically and communicate your ideas. When we are in meetings, you need to provide opinions and contribute. I need to know you have the judgment and tenacity to say something is not a good idea. If I don't see those attributes, I am going to have a hard time putting you in this position. But I want to set you up for success, so these are the things I need to see from you."

This short speech emphasizes affection and direction. Again, consider the equation for how to engage with people: 70% affection, 20% direction, and 10% correction. Giving correction is not the most enjoyable part of the job, but if you are following this pattern, your people can trust that you want them to succeed. With that security they can receive correction and implement it for the betterment of themselves and the company.

Take note, with this concept of two-way confidence it is important I allow my teammates to say, "Hey boss, I want to set you up for success and I think this is a poor decision." Accepting and applying apt constructive criticism will show my team that I respect their opinions, and will undoubtedly build trust.

"What do you think?"

When my team asks my preference, many times I like to get their opinion or let them decide. I might say, "You are closer to the problem; what are your thoughts?" When you give people freedom to decide, then you build their ability and confidence to do so. And that is what leadership is all about. Encourage their critical thought and if appropriate, validate their final response with, "I think that's a great idea. That's the answer I would have chosen as well."

When you are ready to further your mentorship, you can ask deeper questions like, "What do you think the implications of this will be?" When they have to unravel questions that are normally your expertise, they are developing as a future leader. As a bonus, you get a front seat to learn where they excel and where they need more guidance.

It takes time, effort, and money to invest in other people. But the rewards of building a happy and successful team far outweigh any initial investment we could make.

LEADING OTHERS

CONFRONT ISSUES WITHOUT BEING CONFRONTATIONAL

CHAPTER 14

LEADERS CONVEY VALUE WHEN...

THEY PROPERLY ADDRESS UNMET EXPECTATIONS AND ENCOURAGE REHABILITATION.

14. CONFRONT ISSUES WITHOUT BEING CONFRONTATIONAL

People issues are probably a leader's most important—but least favorite—item to deal with. It is not a matter of _if_, but _when_, you will be called on to handle a situation, so it is best to adopt a proper plan and perspective. Unmet expectations must be addressed before they become a distraction to the team. As a leader, you cannot overlook problems, because if you don't fix them, who will? Dealing with problems is not an option—it is your responsibility. People are the greatest asset of your company, and you will find that you spend 90% of your time on 10% of the people. As their leader, you do not have the luxury of ignoring problems.

> *"Conflict aversion is the organizational bubonic plague of our times.*
> *It is cowardice wearing a smart, politically correct hat."*[15]
> — Gus Lee in *Courage*

When expectations are not met, the reason usually falls into one of two categories: skill or will. Either someone was incapable of meeting expectations (skill) or chose not to meet expectations (will). The underlying issues and potential resolutions vary based on the category, so be sure to identify the situation before deciding which tools to use for the ultimate goal of this process, reconciliation.

Skill — Issues of skill can occur because the system is not designed adequately. Another common occurrence is that someone is not adequately prepared to meet the expectation because they do not possess the skills to complete the task. In this instance the supervisor bears the responsibility because the team member did not receive adequate training for the job.

For example, if you work in construction and ask a plumber to shingle the roof, you cannot be upset when your expectations are not met. A plumber is not equipped to complete that task. Clearly, this example is egregious because it is far-fetched to give someone a task in an entirely different area of expertise. But in a business environment, it happens more often than we like to admit.

---

15   (Lee and Elliott-Lee 2010)

When dealing with a situation where expectations were not met, how often do you ask these questions?

- "Did you understand the assignment?"
- "Did you have the tools you needed to complete this task?"
- "Were you trained on this task?"

Ideally, those questions would be asked before you delegated the task, but once the difficulty has occurred, it is irresponsible to hold someone else accountable for your failure to properly assign the task. To resolve the situation, the first step is to take your share of the responsibility and then provide additional training or equipment so your colleague is better prepared for their roles and responsibilities.

Unmet expectations as a result of skill might also occur when a person is experiencing emotional difficulties. As a young captain, I worked in nuclear command and control. One day, one of my troops asked if I would support reprimanding a team member who had not been pulling her weight.

I asked, "What's going on?"

He said, "Well, she is delayed on her work. She works nights, and when I come in on the day shift, her work isn't done or it's sloppy. I have to repeatedly correct it or make her stay so she can do it."

We had twelve-hour shift work, and we had to have the opportunity for eight hours of uninterrupted sleep before our shifts. Our alertness was mandated because of our nuclear requirements. We even had limitations on our self-medication as that would lessen our alertness. Overall, this sleep issue could develop into a pattern, and I foresaw the danger of her eventually violating her crew rest.

He continued, "At the end of her shift, sometimes she has to stay another two hours to finish up the items that she should have been doing already. It's been happening for a while and I'm just frustrated with it. I feel like we need to give her a formal letter of discipline."

This staff sergeant was usually a high performer, and the behavior seemed out of the ordinary.

I asked, "Have you talked to her to see what's going on?"

He reluctantly responded with, "No, ma'am, but I will." He left my office and returned the next morning. He asked to come in, and then he sat down in a chair and began crying.

I asked, "Hey, are you okay?"

He regained his composure and said, "Yes, ma'am. I just want to thank you because I went and talked to the staff sergeant, and I found out that she and her husband were having trouble at home. She was distracted by the issues at home and as a result was not sleeping well, so she was exhausted, and came to work unfocused. That's why she was unproductive. Also, when she was at home, she did not want to be home. She was worried about getting a divorce, what it would do to their young son, and ultimately, how all of this would impact him."

Her supervisor continued, "Here I was, ready to write her paperwork that would impact her permanent file, when all she needed were resources to be able to get help. I've given her the information to connect with lawyers, chaplains, and mental health personnel. She was grateful, and I believe she is going to receive the help she needs so that she can get back on track."

I remember the supervisor's face being so dejected that he was ready to go in guns blazing with only half of the picture in hand. When he took the time to assess the situation and ask a few probing questions, his assessment was 180 degrees different than it had been merely one day before. Our fellow airman was a star performer skilled in competency and capability, but was experiencing an awful season in her life that made her emotionally and mentally unable to meet the tasks at-hand. She wasn't willfully choosing to be unproductive. Instead of reacting to unmet expectations, her supervisor appropriately led her that day.

The situation was a huge learning moment for everyone involved. An exciting end to the story is that the staff sergeant and her husband reconciled, they added a daughter to their family, and eventually she moved on from that assignment to take on a command-and-control mission that supported Air Force One.

This illustration shows why it is so important to understand where your people are coming from. You will never understand if you do not ask questions.

Will — An issue of will occurs when an individual <u>chooses</u> not to follow instructions. The accountability in these instances lies with the individual who made the choice. The consequences usually include discipline and punishment.

When dealing with people after they have failed to meet expectations, remember several important things:

1. Focus on the Process

Ask yourself, "What is my desired outcome?" Effective discipline's main goal should be rehabilitation—you want to prevent the event from happening again. Despite the fact that punishment may be a part of the process, that cannot be the sole focus. You should want someone to become better, not simply make them look or feel bad. What you are trying to do is take something that is broken and put it back together. There are times you are trying to change someone's will, but at the end of the day, you are trying to help someone become better, and help your team to function without the distraction of a teammate who is not in compliance.

2. Emotionally Prepare for the Meeting with Your Colleague

Effective discipline requires commitment to a few ground rules, the first of which is: respond, don't react. Responding means you take the time to understand the situation. You are calm and collected. When you react, you are impulsive and governed solely by feelings. A leader reacting might say things like, "How could you? Why would you do that? What would make you think that was okay?"

If you slow down, step away, and eliminate emotions from the situation, then you can take time to reflect personally. You see that yes, your expectations weren't met, but in reality, things are still okay in the world. If you need to take time before you address your colleague, you can calmly say, "Hey, I need to speak to you about this. We need to talk about it later, but we will take time to sort it out." If you take the time to be rational, it takes emotions out of the equation. It is incredibly important to make sure that you respond, not react.

I made a commitment to myself when I was nineteen years old that I would never discipline while I was angry because of an experience I had at the Air Force Academy. As a freshman, the sophomore cadets were our primary physical trainers, and they would quiz us on our military knowledge during our physical training. One day, we were doing our push-ups, sit-ups, flutter kicks, and all the rest, while reciting the crew compliments of aircraft in the Air Force inventory. One of the trainers—who had never shown any animosity to us before—was very angry, and he made us perform a grueling workout with increased repetitions and sets. His tone was incredibly harsh and he berated us for minor mistakes. It was uncharacteristic, and I remember later learning that his girlfriend had broken up with him over the weekend. His bad day became everyone's bad day when he began taking it out on the rest of us. It was at that moment that I remember committing to myself, "I will never discipline when I am angry."

As a leader, it is important to think about how a person responds to discipline. If this is the first instance of discipline and you have no baseline, think about their characteristics and traits. Are they incredibly sensitive and aware of the fact that they have failed to meet expectations? Perhaps that will drive you to have a clear, short discussion about how to move forward. Maybe you just need to tell them, "Hey, I'm really disappointed, please do better next time," and that will solve the problem immediately. If they are angry and do not feel that they did anything wrong, it may take more time and teaching to explain the realities of the situation.

Is the individual prone to yelling in response? Do you anticipate they are going to try to twist your words or take them out of context? This lends itself to the final recommendation about the environment—ensure you have another person in the room with you. This recommendation is so that you have a third-party witness to the conversation. Another person will provide a level of security in case tensions are out of control and they can deter false accusations in the future. Most of the time, this additional person would be the employee's direct supervisor, but who do you bring in if the employee is your direct report? While I would not recommend bringing one of their peers, you can bring in one of your peers, someone who is at your same level administratively, or as a last resort, someone who supervises both of you.

3. Physically Prepare for the Meeting with Your Colleague

Praise in public, punish in private. The location where you handle your discipline is incredibly important. If you determine that you need to talk to somebody about their behavior and their conduct, make sure that you're doing it in a private area where all parties can participate and speak freely. Do not add extra embarrassment and compound the difficulty of the situation by creating a scene.

One small caveat to the privacy rule occurs when "spot corrections" are necessary. These are the mistakes that must be corrected quickly, no matter where you are. For example:

- "Hey, put your hard hat on."
- "Use a ladder."
- "We don't talk like that."
- "That joke is not acceptable here."

If you determine that a private conversation is warranted, be conscious about the environment of the room in which you are planning to meet. When sensitivity or a light hand is called for, you might need a room where you can sit next to the person and reassure them. In a more hostile environment, you might sit with a barrier, such as a desk, between you. In the event the person becomes violent or angry, a barrier might prevent a physical altercation. It is important to set the environment in a way that allows you to achieve your objective.

Consider stocking the room with tissues and a bottle of water, or anything that could provide creature comforts in the middle of a difficult time. As they are receiving correction, they may feel hurt, angry, or a myriad of emotions. Tears could flow or they could get choked up and have a dry throat, so be prepared for those scenarios.

The timing of the meeting is also important. Do not allow too much time between the infraction and your conversation, otherwise the overall impact is lessened. After you become aware of an issue, I recommend dealing with it within 24 hours (i.e., one work day), and no later than 48 hours (i.e., two work days).

Provide discipline early in the work day, if able, so you have time to check on them before the end of the day and ensure they are in the proper frame of mind. Imagine a situation where you dole out discipline on a Friday and you won't see that person until Monday. If someone is underperforming at work and perhaps has other personal issues as well, there are two days without contact with them. Monday morning you expect them to come to work, but what happens if they do things out of character? What if they binge drink? Or what happens if they start to make poor decisions, they drive too fast, they do something harmful to themselves or to others in their home? There is no opportunity for you to check on them between that Friday afternoon and that Monday. Also, if you administer discipline at the end of the day, then you still have an additional 18 hours before you see them again the next day. I strongly recommend disciplining in the morning and having a check-in at the end of the day.

While you are not responsible for your teammate's personal choices, a responsible leader takes steps that will hopefully prevent someone from making bad decisions on their personal time because they are upset about a conflict at work. Disciplining early in the day allows for a natural cooling off period, while an end-of-day check-in allows you to check in on their mental state before they go home for the evening or weekend (more information to follow on this process).

4. Prepare for Two-Way Communication

Questions stir the conscience; accusations harden the will. Always seek to listen. Heavy-handed discipline is a very hard thing to sit through as a child and even harder as an adult. Listening to accusations can be demoralizing and demeaning. For example:

- "You did this, and it was wrong! This is the third time you were late this week."
- "This is frustrating, and you have to do better."

However, if you ask questions instead of accusing, you will go further with people. When people feel they can share their side of a story, they will feel more comfortable. To begin a meeting, I find the following phrases helpful to address the issue and open a line of communication:

- "Tell me about what happened back there."
- "This is what I know. Can you fill me in on why you made that decision?"
- "I saw that this happened and I didn't understand. Can you explain this to me?"
- "What happened was clearly against the rules. But can you tell me what you understood the rules to be?"

This technique of asking questions is a "win" for both of you. You get more information about the situation and them as a person. Also, you allow them to participate in the process as opposed to it being a monologue from the boss.

As you communicate, remember what you want to accomplish and how you want that person to feel when they walk out of the room. Tailor your meeting and words to that end. Do you want a rehabilitated member to reengage with the team? Do you want somebody who is ready to come back to tackle the mission? Is it a "shot across the bow" and you just need to have a stern conversation? Clearly communicate the unmet expectation and the expected conduct.

- "This happened, it cannot happen again."
- "You have made jokes like this and they are inappropriate."
- "You're making people feel uncomfortable."
- "These are the things that you cannot do, and I cannot allow."

5. Document Your Conversations

Prepare for future communication: document, document, document. It is very important for you to keep a summary record of the discipline session. Some institutions even require these "records of conversation" in order to move forward with employee evaluation decisions. I recommend that as soon as the person leaves your office you jot down a few quick notes on a Word document. You might decide that an official memorandum or an official "record of conversation" is appropriate and will become part of an employee's record; other times that won't be necessary. Take these documents and store them in a secure file on your computer. This will prevent your colleague from saying, "I never received any corrections about that topic," or, "No one ever told me this was an area of concern."

You can bring these documents when you need to communicate with human resources and can share, "I talked to this person on three separate occasions about X, Y, or Z, and they still haven't adjusted their behavior." These documents do not need to be published, emailed, or public, though they can be if it becomes apparent that they should. They do not even need to include great detail, but you need to write some of the key highlights. For example, "I talked to this person about this issue on this date. They responded with this. They said this was the rationale." Those notes will be helpful when you are writing summaries, submitting annual reports, evaluating salary increase requests, compiling progress reports, and more. When expectations are unmet, make sure that you document not only for your sake, but also for the other person's sake.

6. Ensure Mutual Understanding of Your Desired End State

If rehabilitation is your ultimate goal for someone, it is important that they are ready to return without any tension or hard feelings. In an ideal situation each party agrees that the conversation was both necessary and productive. One way to help smooth any rough edges is to follow up with them before the end of the day. At the end of the meeting say, "Hey, before we leave today, I'd like to check in with you. Stop back around four o'clock because I just want to catch up one more time."

In the military, we have a positive hand-off buddy system that ensures someone escorts a person back to their unit after a difficult meeting. That is a good practice in an office setting, too. Perhaps someone from HR or a senior member on your team can walk them back to their station so there is someone they can talk to or debrief with—or even just have an emotional "sigh" with. As we all know, taking correction is not easy. Your hope is the team member will feel valued instead of punished, and realize that you cared enough to guide them back to the correct course.

During the follow-up meeting later in the day, I recommend saying something like, "Earlier today we had a good conversation. I felt like I understood what your thoughts were. I wanted to follow up and see if you had any questions about anything we've talked about today." If they don't have any questions, you can end it with a simple, "I just want to let you know you're a valued member of this team, and if there's anything you need, let me know. But otherwise, I look forward to seeing you continue to make progress."

If you had to use the "shot across the bow" approach, you can say, "Hey, thanks for checking in. I know that was a hard conversation to hear today. I appreciate you sharing, but I want to make sure that the line is kept. If there's anything else that you wanted to share in the meantime, please let me know. Otherwise, I look forward to seeing you tomorrow."

With thoughtful consideration and planning, it is possible to confront issues without being confrontational. You must not look at discipline as confrontation, but rather reconciliation. You are trying to take something that is broken and put it back together, whether it's an unmet expectation, a willful disobedience, or a struggle to grow and become better. You cannot overlook problems because you are the final stop. If you don't fix it, who will?

LEADING OTHERS

RUN EFFECTIVE MEETINGS

CHAPTER 15

LEADERS CONVEY VALUE WHEN...

THEY STEWARD TIME WISELY BY CONDUCTING PRODUCTIVE MEETINGS.

15. RUN EFFECTIVE MEETINGS

Meetings. Are. The. Biggest. Waste. Of. Time. There, I said it. Ineffective meetings reflect ineffective leadership.

Studies show employees spend an average of 31 hours per month in meetings, and 50% of that time is considered wasted.[16] If you are anything like me, the time after a meeting is spent on "after-meeting meetings" when I connect with colleagues to ask about tasks or concepts that were unclear in the original meeting. We converse, and then I try to catch another colleague to clear up concepts from their arena as well. Basically, the team spends an hour in a group meeting, then another hour finding answers the original meeting was supposed to provide. Do you see the problem?

Ineffective meetings waste time and money and cause frustration. (I will admit, sometimes for fun, I tally the amount of money being spent on salaries for senior leadership to sit in a one-hour meeting that does nothing to further the cause.)

So, if we schedule a meeting, we must ensure the following:

Every Meeting Must Have a Leader

Take charge of your meeting. Do not allow sidebar conversations or meandering rabbit trails. Keep the meeting on track within the designated time limits. Maintain clear transitions from topic to topic, and ensure everyone has an opportunity to provide input. After input is incorporated, be clear about the decision made. Guide the discussion and do not allow one person to overtake the conversation. The goal of a meeting is an efficient exchange of information, and we as leaders control whether this happens or not.

Every Meeting Must Have a Goal

Think through the purpose of the meeting, and provide it plainly. The goal of the meeting should be very clear (for example, the C-suite should approve the fourth quarter budget). If there is no purpose to meet, do not have a meeting. If aimless meetings become a chronic issue, it is a frustration (and thus, a

---

16   (Zippia 2023)

distraction) to teammates who want to maximize their productivity while on the clock. Value others by respecting their time.

Every Meeting Must Have the Right People in the Room

Have you ever sat in a meeting and wondered, "Why exactly am I here?" I have. Only decision makers who can provide relevant input should be present. If someone is bringing a mentee, that is fine, but meetings should largely be limited to key personnel.

Every Meeting Must Have an Agenda

An agenda delineates a schedule of topics arranged in the order of discussion and is distributed to meeting attendees. The agenda items should be related to the subject matter at-hand, and the leader should not wander into off-topic areas. When you provide an agenda, you show that you have thought through what to discuss.

If my team and I find ourselves delving into topics that are out of the scope of the meeting, we use the term "parking lot" to convey that the information would be recorded and brought up for discussion at a later time, sometimes even in a later meeting.

Every Meeting Should Consider Using Read-Aheads

A read-ahead is a document reviewed before the meeting. If there are charts, graphs, or anything that requires teams to review and present their opinion, people should have access to the document at least twenty-four hours before the meeting.

It is a waste of time to have everyone in the room read a document, and then expect the team to provide their instantaneous feedback on it. People absorb information at different speeds, and people form opinions at different speeds. When I am providing my opinion, I like to analyze all aspects of the decision verbally. I noticed that I missed out on hearing people's thoughts because some people prefer to absorb the information and then provide their thoughts after digesting it. I would be busy talking through my thoughts while others were still forming their opinion in their minds. I was a distraction. However, if I had a read-ahead, I would have spent the time processing my opinion, and come to the meeting ready to discuss. This is the key benefit of a read-ahead: people can process information and form an opinion before the meeting. Not every meeting requires a read-ahead, but they should be a consideration for every meeting.

Every Meeting Must Have a Time Limit

This notion is not cosmic, but it is a common struggle with leaders who want to keep their meetings brief. Someone asked me how they could make their meetings shorter, and I suggested blocking off less time on the clock, and scheduling other items around it on the calendar. These constraints encourage both focus and a streamlined approach to meeting the goal.

Every Meeting Must Have a Designated Recorder

For consistency's sake, the recorder should be the person who sends out the invites to the meetings. The recorder should provide the read-aheads, goal, and agenda when sending the invitation. They list detailed information on the type of meeting it will be, the duration, and if anything is required beforehand. They also send out a same-day summary report with consolidation of tasks and developed timelines.

Oftentimes in meetings, leaders will throw out unassigned tasks. For example, "I need three proposals for marketing agencies." Then, they will move onto the next item on the agenda. At this point, no one is accountable for completing that task, and either an expectation will be unmet, or in an incredibly ambitious situation, multiple people will think they are responsible for it, and will get frustrated when they later find out their work was needless since the task was also completed by someone else.

When providing a task, be specific with the task, the person, and the timeline. Be sure to confirm the timeline with the person completing the task.

Natasha (Leader): "Lacey, I need three proposals for marketing agencies. Can you get that list to me by Tuesday at 4:00?"

Lacey: "I can't do Tuesday at 4:00 p.m., but I can do Wednesday at 9:00 a.m."

Natasha: "Great, I'll look for it in my inbox on Wednesday morning."

At this point, the recorder writes down Lacey's responsibility and the due date. The recorder plays a crucial role in ensuring no task falls through the cracks. They eliminate questions and the need for people to mill about after meetings trying to remember what they discussed.

Here are four meeting types I hold, how often I have them, and the estimated time for each:

- **Strategic: The "Why/Vision"**
  Frequency: Biweekly
  Length: 30-60 minutes
  Attendees: Strategic leaders (C-suite executives)
  Goal: Decide if a decision is aligned with strategic goals

  Example: We are going to host a family day to show our appreciation for our workers and their families.

- **Operational: The "How/Mission"**
  Frequency: Weekly
  Length: 30 minutes
  Attendees: Mid-level management
  Goal: Hand out roles and responsibilities

  Example: We need to book a location, have something fun for the kids, and provide food. Finance team, what is a reasonable budget? Operations team, you are accountable for making sure items are purchased within the budget limits.

- **Tactical: The "What/Goals"**
  Frequency: Every other day
  Length: 20 minutes
  Attendees: Pertinent team members
  Goal: Provide clear instructions about tasks.

  Example: The Operations team determines the event will be held in the company parking lot, and a bouncy castle will be present. Hot dogs, hamburgers, chips, and sodas will be served.

- **Administrative: Updates/Questions**
  Frequency: Daily
  Length: 5-15 minutes
  Attendees: Workers
  Goal: Quick check-in on the status

  Example: The members of the Operations team assigned to the food portion of the event connect to keep each other apprised and address any problems.

  I often refer to this meeting as a "stand-up," because the team stands up throughout it, ensuring a quicker meeting. The agenda for this meeting is simply the issues of the previous day.

These streamlined meetings bring only necessary teammates to the table, allowing us to speak about things specific to that group. The meetings stay organized and on schedule, which is vital to the efficiency of our team's time and energy.

Visit battleprovenleadership.com/book-resources to download a sample meeting readahead.

The RACI Matrix

People need structure. When you give them structure, then direct them to their lane and teach them how to think critically, you have given them the tools to succeed.

I use a popular management model called the RACI Matrix to effectively keep track of my team's roles and responsibilities for each project. Edmond F. Sheehan developed the RACI Matrix in the 1950s, and countless organizations adopted the technique over the decades.

Here is the breakdown of the RACI model in its basic form:

- Responsible: person/people who do the task
- Accountable: person who ensures task completion
- Consulted: person/people who must provide input
- Informed: person/people who need to know

Using this model in chart form allows you to see who is involved in each stage; it keeps everything organized and streamlined. My teams enjoy knowing exactly what's expected of them and having the freedom to perform their jobs without hindrance. This is a document that you develop in an operational meeting as you determine the tasks, and assign accountable parties. In the tactical meeting you assign the responsible parties.

Notice that every task has one person assigned as accountable. This person may not be the person who will complete the task (that is the responsible party); however, this is the sole person who will communicate with the leader about progress reports and task completion. Take the example of my former colleague who I asked to provide a slide show update, and I did not provide customized leadership. Although there were several people who were responsible for providing information for the slide show, at the end of the day, he was the one who I would ask about the finished product.

If you want effective meetings that don't waste your or your team's time, the RACI model can be a valuable tool. But whether you try this method or another, I highly recommend having a tool to keep everyone organized and your tasks on track.

Visit battleprovenleadership.com/book-resources to download a sample RACI chart.

FINAL THOUGHTS

Leadership is an art that requires practice.

If you read ten leadership books, it is likely you would learn ten different philosophies. And that is to be expected—each leader brings something different to the table. This book features the tools I have gathered over decades of serving leaders and serving as a leader.

I am not a subject expert, but rather a practitioner. As I practice the art of leadership, I continue to be inquisitive and humbly committed to learning to become a better leader. Each day and situation I encounter offers the chance to test my philosophy and hone my skills. I have tried and tested these techniques and wholeheartedly endorse them; however, it is true that your situation and skillset may require you to tweak certain aspects to fit your team. You should trust yourself to find what works best for your people.

Leadership can feel like an overwhelming task, but all you should ask of yourself is that you consistently work toward being better. There is a saying some attribute to a man named George Fulton that I find particularly poignant: "Success is not final, failure is not fatal; it is the courage to continue that counts."[17] Give all you have toward the people you are assigned to work alongside and you are going to be successful.

Let me leave you with this quote and a bit of encouragement: Jim Kwik says, "On the days you only have 40% and you give 40%, you gave 100%."[18] I have encouraged you to do better and be better, and if you give all you have to give each day, then you did exactly what was expected of you.

Finally, I'd like to challenge you with those who have impacted my life in an incredible way...

---

17   (Tilton 1948)
18   (Kwik 2022)

LEADERSHIP
HALL OF FAME

SMSgt Paul R. Green Jr., USAF – A leader who builds confidence in others. My Poppa always told me how smart I was and how beautiful I was. He always emphasized my talents and was always ready to teach me how to do new things—everything from sports to public speaking. He never let me say, "I can't." My confidence in God's ability to use me was bred through my Poppa's confidence in me.

Vivian M. Green – A leader who serves with all of her energy. My Momma is always finding ways to make people's lives easier; whether that is inviting people to live in our home who need help, or finding ways to help around each of her adult children's houses, her acts of service always show her love. We had exchange students, exchange teachers, and others join our household. She always cooked more than enough to invite anyone who wanted to come. Everyone knows Momma Green will always be available to help.

Dr. John Wilkerson (Pastor) – A leader who leads by example. His humility, consistent willingness and readiness to provide compassion and grace, show me the love of Christ. You know that his decisions are trustworthy because he lives for an audience of One.

Linda Wilkerson (Pastor's wife) – A leader who extends compassion and commits to meeting people where they are. Her down-to-earth nature is an example from which to learn. She is ready to challenge me with the hard questions and always has time for me.

Dr. Michael Rodgers (Childhood pastor) – A leader who communicates potential. Vision is the ability to see what others cannot and what does not exist at the moment. For decades, he has believed there are no limits to my opportunities, and he has never hesitated to tell anyone else who would listen. His confidence in me is a great encouragement.

Mark Maxwell (Youth pastor) – A leader who invests in my growth. I interacted and engaged with him multiple times a week at church. He provided clear truths in an understandable way. He never sugarcoated the truth, and accelerated my love for living for Christ.

Ali Maxwell (Youth pastor's wife) – A leader who listens. She always listens to me with great interest and lovingly points me back to Christ. She never makes me feel as if my feelings are invalid, and will always tell me the truth, with a spirit of restoration. She allows her house to be a respite and a refuge where I can be authentic, and I always feel welcome.

Dr. Bob Green – A leader who leads with Christ-like love. Uncle Bob is a trailblazing, missionary aviator who believed in the MissionAero Pipeline before it became a reality. He invested his time, talent, and treasure to jumpstart a program that develops and serves missionaries through aviation. He and Aunt Patsy consistently show love to everyone they encounter. His continuous mentorship and solid character are exemplary.

Dr. Mark Bosje – A leader who understands balance. He focuses on the mission and the people, with a unique balance so that each entity receives the value it deserves. He does an excellent job of opening doors for people to thrive, and trusts people to handle their tasks. He rescued me and allowed me to dream big when I was at an impasse.

Tim Edson (Political consultant) – A leader who fights for his people. When the political reporter called him for my commentary about my sexual assault, he fought tooth and nail for my right to privacy as a victim. When he broke the news to me that the press was going to publish it, he made sure I had the opportunity to share my truth both in the article and on national media. He also prepared me for the media barrage. He fought for me, and with me, during one of the hardest battles I've ever faced. He is a wingman with the same dedication I found on the battlefield during combat.

General Ondra Berry, USAF – A leader who builds other leaders. He conveys value to every single person he encounters. When I finish speaking with him, I have confidence that I can be, and do, anything in the world. He mentors anyone who wants to learn, and executes at a level of excellence, with a clear push to mentor and model his expectations.

General E. John "Dragon" Teichert, USAF – A leader who models excellence and humility. A man who stands up for his beliefs without fear of consequence. He takes the time to answer my questions about my environment, and builds my leadership with a customized approach.

General Dana Nelson, USAF – A leader who makes time for others and provides a safe environment to ask questions. She is a clear example that rank determines pay grade, but humanity is what makes the difference as a leader.

General Felicia Brokaw, USA – A leader who is present. She intentionally seeks to say people's names in rooms of opportunity, and she understands the value a leader's presence brings to the overall success of an event.

General Michael Stohler, USAF – A leader who leads with compassion. People are not items on his to-do list. When George Floyd was murdered in 2020, I saw him agonize over ensuring he conveyed a meaningful message to the team. He took input and adjusted to bring our team through a tough time in a unified manner.

 Special Agent/Colonel Bridget Graham, USAF – A leader who leads with boldness. When I shared with her the details of the initial assault and the handling of it, she said, "I believe you. This is wrong." She will boldly share the truth, and will fight to ensure wrongs are righted. She has a unique way of saying the hard things but leaving you with a clear view of the situation. (Due to her military activities, I am respectfully refraining from publishing her photo.)

 Colonel Tami Saylor, USAF – A leader who challenges others to grow. I was sitting in my office when she stopped in to share that I should consider becoming a military commander. She alleviated my fears and conveyed that my leadership was needed by our organization. I stepped outside of my comfort zone and it has changed my trajectory for the better.

 Colonel Timothy Donofrio, USAF – A leader who exemplifies customized leadership. An introvert with high expectations, he encouraged me to strive to do more, without ever making me feel pressured. He guided me with my command decisions, and it is an honor when he shares that he is proud of me.

 Colonel Kyle Noel, USAF – A leader who cares. I had a medical issue which required the Air Force to evaluate my suitability to serve. He called me and said, "I want you to know we [leadership] are in your corner. We want you to stay and we will fight to make that happen." I felt valued. I felt seen. I aim to value and see people today because of his example.

Captain Antionette Cox – A leader who mentors. I was a late bloomer at USAFA, not fully understanding how to be effective in that space. She met with me biweekly and redirected me from a path of failure to a path of success. She believed in me and spent time helping me develop. I would not have graduated from USAFA without her.

Chief Kerry Ghent, USAF – A leader who led me as he followed me. From the start of my military career at USAFA, I have always heard to latch onto a senior non-commissioned officer, and learn from them. Chief was that person for me. He challenged me to think with these two sentences often, "Ma'am, is that a hill you want to die on?" and "Ma'am, I will follow whichever direction you go, but this is a bad decision." I learned who I was, how I was perceived, and how I could be more effective through his leadership and guidance.

BIBLIOGRAPHY

1. Angelou, Maya, and Oprah Winfrey. (1969) 2015. *I Know Why the Caged Bird Sings.* New York: Random House.

2. Grenier, Richard. "Perils of Passive Sex," *The Washington Times,* April 6, 1993.

3. Jeremiah, David. 2004. *Searching for Heaven on Earth Journal.* Integrity Publishing.

4. Powell, Colin L., and Joseph E. Persico. 2003. *My American Journey.* New York: Ballantine Books.

5. Causey, Charles. 2018. *Words and Deeds: Becoming a Man of Courageous Integrity.* Colorado Springs, CO: NavPress.

6. Sanborn, Mark. 2006. *You Don't Need a Title to Be a Leader: How Anyone, Anywhere, Can Make a Positive Difference.* New York: Currency Doubleday.

7. Your Story "Lead with Action, Not Words: The Narayana Murthy Guide." YourStory.com, September 20, 2023. https://yourstory.com/2023/09/leadership-example-narayana-murthy-insights.

8. Gordon, Jon. 2015. *You Win in the Locker Room First: 7 C's to Build a Winning Team in Sports, Business and Life.* Hoboken, N.J.: Wiley.

9. Hung, Carl. 2021. *"Council Post: Crisis Decision-Making: How Company Values Can Guide the Way."* Forbes. April 2, 2021. https://www.forbes.com/sites/forbesbusinesscouncil/2021/04/02/crisis-decision-making-how-company-values-can-guide-the-way/?sh=731ebd2b10f8.

10. Iacocca, Lee. 1984. *Iacocca: An autobiography.* Toronto; New York: Bantam Books.

11. York, Daniel. 2017. *The Strong Leader's Hand: 6 Essential Elements Every Leader Must Master.* Ishpeming, Mich.: Book Venture Publishing LLC.

12. Ruggeri, Amanda. *"Jim Sinegal: Costco CEO Focuses on Employees."* U.S. News, October 22, 2009. https://www.usnews.com/news/leaders.

13. Blanchard, Ken. 2009. "Feedback Is the Breakfast of Champions." Ken Blanchard Books (blog). August 17, 2009. https://www.kenblanchardbooks.com/feedback-is-the-breakfast-of-champions/.

14. Campbell, Capt. Chris. to Jennifer-Ruth Green. n.d. Face-to-face.

15. Lee, Gus, and Diane Elliott-Lee. 2010. *Courage.* John Wiley & Sons.

16. 28+ incredible meeting statistics [2023]: Virtual, Zoom, in-person meetings and productivity. Zippia. (2023, July 7). https://www.zippia.com/advice/meeting-statistics/

17. Tilton, George. 1948. "Thoughts on the Business of Life." *Forbes,* November 1, 1948.

18. Kwik, Jim [@jimkwik]. (2022, October 17). On the days you only have 40%, and you give 40%, you gave 100%. [Tweet]. Twitter.

View additional resources from Jennifer-Ruth Green and Battle-Proven Leadership at
BATTLEPROVENLEADERSHIP.COM

Made in the USA
Monee, IL
13 February 2024

52914254R00089